2017

To Cla
... who una~
the PATH!

♥

Nancy

# Shirt Tales

*The Stories behind a Successful Start-up*

NANCY GOLD

ISBN: 978-1-4834-5763-5 (sc)
ISBN: 978-1-4834-5764-2 (e)  ·

Library of Congress Control Number: 2016914499

Lulu Publishing Services rev. date: 09/27/2016

# About the Author

**Nancy Gold, Entrepreneur**
*Photo by Sarah R. Bloom*

Nancy Gold is a Master Shirtmaker, Business Writer and Entrepreneurial Coach and serves as President of King's Collar Shirtmakers Inc., and its divisions TKC Business Consultants and The King's Writer. She has been honored as an *INC. Magazine* "Entrepreneur of the Year" and is a *Pennsylvania's Best 50 Women in Business* recipient. She has been a business advocate and a community activist since the 1980s and has worked within the marginalized community for positive change. Nancy Gold is a Founder of Philadelphia's Center City District and has raised over one million dollars for community projects. She is a voice-over artist, and as President of Philadelphia's Center City Proprietors Association and The Ardmore Business Association, has worked with hundreds of small businesses to help shape their message. Hired by The Custom Shop in 1965, she is the first woman in the country to evolve as a Custom Shirtmaker in this male-dominated industry. Nancy has five children and five grandchildren and lives in Ardmore, PA.

# Advance Praise

Tenacity. Perseverance. Success and Failure. The real life lessons of starting and succeeding at business are brought home in Nancy Gold's 50-year journey to making King's Collar Shirtmakers, Inc. the success it is today. It is a must for anyone who is starting a business and wants to go into it with their eyes wide open.

—Drew Katz, CEO, *Interstate Outdoor Advertising*, Founder and CEO of *The Rachel and Drew Katz Foundation*

=========================================================

Nancy Gold in her book SHIRT TALES takes us through the successful journey of a pioneer entrepreneur. Nancy's journey is not only one of a successful business woman, but that of an impact player in a city of leaders. Her narrative is a must read, not only for those seeking success in business, but for those seeking to make a difference in the larger community:

Nancy Gold is a model for those seeking to do so.

Dr. W. Wilson Goode, Sr.
Former Mayor – City of Philadelphia
(1984-1992)

=========================================================

*SHIRT TALES* tracks the climb of a local start-up and a wise guide for those considering this exciting possibility. Proprietor-owned businesses are the engines that drive a city and Nancy's story is a model of resilience within a telling portrait of Center City's remarkable growth. Plus, it's a nostalgic ride for those of us who were there.

—Meryl Levitz, President and CEO, VISIT PHILADELPHIA.

============================================================

In *Shirt Tales*, Nancy has given us the gift of a brilliantly useful and engaging business book. But *Shirt Tales* is more than just another great business book. It's an engaging and thoughtful story of personal innovation, dogged perseverance and an ultimate commitment to succeed. Nancy's legacy as an icon and pioneer in the custom apparel business is without question. But beyond that, her innate ability to connect with people while serving her community in the spirit of 'repairing the world' one small step at a time is what makes her such an extraordinary human being and valued friend.

Joe Blair
President
Individualized Apparel Group

============================================================

Nancy Gold beautifully shares how she has overcome an ocean of circumstances to become a successful entrepreneur. Her wisdom is a goldmine for anyone who is ready to take that first big step to start their own business.

Pontish Yeramyan
Founder and CEO, Gap International, Inc.

============================================================

# Dedication

I dedicate this book to my sister Rachel Kaplan who loves me unconditionally, and to my sister Joan Peterdi, who took the time to copy edit this material and whose presence in my life continues to support and nourish me.

To my children Steve, Ira, Bob, Mitchell and Lisa and grandchildren John, Logan, Parker, Rya and Grayson; may you now see a different side of me and understand how it shapes the lives we share.

—Everything I do is for you.

# Acknowledgment

This book is filled with the names of people who served as mentors, clients, family and friends, and I am humbled by their contributions. I'm especially thankful to my friend Rennie Cohen who suggested the recap format for each chapter ending, and double thanks to my sister Joan who kept me on the writing path with meaningful suggestions that became part of the final manuscript.

I have also tracked this journey for those who aspire to be the drivers of their own lives. It's sometimes risky, often scary, but the path untraveled goes *nowhere*.

"I am the master of my fate:
I am the captain of my soul."
— **William Ernest Henley**, **Invictus**

# Contents

# Foreword

The book you are about to read has been written by a woman who exemplified the term *start-up* long before the term evolved. She presents a panoramic cinema-graphic view "in living color" of the birth of a business, rooted in a childhood memory, that evolved into a fifty-year journey.

To know this author as I do is to recognize how her positive view has touched hundreds of lives. While there are many *how-to* books that lay out steps to follow, Nancy Gold reveals the insights she gained in real-time by actual breakthroughs and break-downs that later become a *how I did it* book positioned to encourage others to "go for it."

The writing is conversational, almost as though she is speaking directly to you, peppered with gems of wisdom that can help others avoid some of the pitfalls she encountered. As a professional speech writer and editorialist, Nancy's narrative flows easily and engages the reader by first sharing a story and then highlighting the lesson learned. To read the bolded insights and chapter recaps is in itself useful as one could never extrapolate the material supporting them; a chronological tale, each step naturally grows out of the previous one—often by surprise. *Shirt Tales* offers a road map and a point of view that few business books are able to share

There is a pervasive underlying theme in the narrative, subtle enough to keep the story interesting yet unexplainable unless one believes in a higher power directing coincidences of timing. The author stresses the importance for her of having faith that a positive outcome will follow any roadblock, and by inference, offers this as meaningful for other aspiring entrepreneurs.

While the book speaks to a successful retail story, the bonus *Business Manual* is easily adapted for any new business venture. If you're considering an idea that could lead to a business, the steps presented here could pave the way to success because the shared insights that led to its writing have solid professional value.

The author is well-known within the business community as someone with grit and purpose. A *pit bull* when she's on a quest to achieve a positive outcome, she is authentic in her day to day interactions, allowing her to attract and work with people from every social stratum. Today, we call this *networking* but for Nancy Gold it's always been an operating principle.

*Shirt Tales* is a book defined by its author; a reflection of her life mantra, the book is indeed *"Fabulous!"*

She is, after all, "our Nancy Gold" — a "little shot" who created a formula for interacting with the "big shots" who partnered with her in growing her company. Over the years, her energy and authenticity continue to prevail.

On the beach or by the fire, a good read anywhere!

No entrepreneur should be without it. Well done!

Eugene D. McGurk, Jr. Esq.
Cinnaminson, New Jersey

**Eugene D. McGurk** is *Of Counsel*, Raynes McCarty Law Offices. He is Chair, Board of Advisers, Delaware Law School, Widener University and Secretary of the Board of Trustees, Widener University. He is a friend, colleague, and client of the author.

http://raynesmccarty.com/attorneys/eugene-d-mcgurk-jr

# Introduction

Are you considering a life change? Does the thought of being your own boss excite you? What are your strengths? I was unaware of my own until I got tested but adversity can be life's greatest teacher when your only choices are passing or failing. What's needed is a *catalyst* to push you forward, and I trust this book may help fulfill that purpose.

As a young single parent with no college degree, I was hardly on the fast track to business success when I got my first job in 1965. This book describes my first baby steps and how each step since that time shaped my future and changed my life.

My name is Nancy Gold and I'm a Master Shirtmaker. As President and CEO of my own company, I've also consulted with hundreds of other small businesses over the years and I've learned to respect and champion the entrepreneurial drive. I know what it takes to get a new business in place and to be proactive about early start-up pitfalls. The King's Collar Shirtmakers which I founded in 1978, continues to thrive as a small business to this day, but the road taken was strewn with missteps as well as successes. Along the way, I explored ideas and strategies that helped make this path easier to travel, and this book shares some of the insights that worked, as well as some of those that did not.

The book you are about to read began as a manual to help a new business start well and continue with confidence; but as I was writing it, I noticed that the content was coming from a rich vein of other material and personal experiences that shaped my career. I became aware that simply writing a *how-to* book on starting a business would have no *gravitas* unless connected to the break-downs that also occurred along the way and the actual stories about people who helped me, scared me, and ultimately walked with me on a life path that was unimaginable until I began the journey.

*The Business Manual* is now an Appendix at the back of the book, a distillation of everything I learned that ultimately built my company. It can provide solid, professional information and may greatly assist others as they consider this exciting new life path.

Not all can start a business; it's risky and it's not for everyone. Some people want that great job that pays a good salary every week, and hopefully, a year-end bonus commensurate with their talent.

They want something they can depend on, a salary that doesn't change, and a life that's predictable.

That's the person I want to HIRE.

You'll note that my focus is Retail, but whether you're considering a Service Business or a Retail Operation, this book is filled with insights that may resonate with you. **I've bolded the print**, as the **insights** occurred during the writing.

This is a book that honors the entrepreneurial spirit and the start-ups that bring new energy to the workforce. If you're ready to unleash your entrepreneurial talents, you'll be joining an army of people who work hard every day to create jobs for others.

We are the gladiators; our drive, passion and talents make a difference in our communities, and our efforts are notable. We matter.

If you've been led to this book, you may be one of the creative thinkers ready to step outside their comfort zone and I'm happy to join you on that ledge.

***

CHAPTER

# Go for It!

As a youngster, all I wanted was to get through school with dignity, get married, move to the suburbs, and raise kids. I was from the generation where you married young after grooming yourself to attract the hottie who would take care of you until the kids left for college, and then the plan was to retire together in comfort.

I was engaged at sixteen and married at eighteen, but several years later, I was suddenly on my own. The piece of this dream that included marriage and children got accomplished, but the divorce was unexpected; financial support was scarce, and I had no fallback plan. Given my early start, I never completed college, and at age twenty-three, I was raising three children under the age of four— without child support.

Now what?

I was too proud to tell my folks I had failed and too poor to properly care for my children. I was able to sell my jewelry and use the balance of an accident settlement to get money for living expenses, but every week was a challenge. I learned to use powdered milk and stretch my weekly food budget of twenty-five dollars to cover the needs of my young family. (Please note, as this story continues, the money earned or spent, reflects its value at the time.)

In an effort to limit all unnecessary expenses, I kept our heat low, turned my lights off when not needed, and even cancelled my daily paper. And that's how my career actually started. I opened my door one Sunday morning to find a *Philadelphia Inquirer* that had been left there by mistake. Almost by design, I checked the help-wanted section.

In the 1960s, jobs for men and women were listed separately, and in 1965, I found myself guided to an ad that was placed in both sections: *M/F, upscale retail haberdashery sales position now open, $60.00 to $110.00 weekly. Call for interview.*

I just assumed I'd be going for the one hundred and ten dollars a week—considered a good salary in 1965. (By 2016 standards, this would represent almost seven hundred and fifty dollars per week.) Looking back on the actual wording of the ad, I realize that even then I was looking at the glass as half-*full*. It's what I do, and without knowing it at the time, I was exercising one of the attitudes necessary for anyone considering an entrepreneurial endeavor.

**No enterprise should even consider a start-up plan if coming from "the glass is half-empty" point of view.** From the moment one decides to take this step into the unknown, one needs to hold on to the thoughts and actions that reflect a positive attitude, an outrageous drive to succeed, and—balls.

It's also important to keep in mind that the path to owning a company is strewn with the closed businesses of those who neglected to seek out good coaching, gave up too easily, and allowed their egos to run their checkbooks.

This was my maiden voyage into the sea of business, and all I had working for me was the drive (and need) to make money and the unbridled feeling of *possibility*. It was the only ad that caught my attention because I had no training in any field, and I immediately thought, "This is a job I can do!"

I called the number and noted it was with The Custom Shop, a national custom shirt chain of some renown that operated many years ago. My interview was with Alan Bresnick, the personnel manager, who had come to Philadelphia from their flagship store on Fifth Avenue in New York. He explained to me that the men's apparel industry was changing, and he felt there was a place in it for women. I asked him what the job required, and he said I'd be selling neckwear and accessories at the 1700 Walnut Street location in Center City, Philadelphia. It was a six-day job, nine to six, but Wednesday's were nine to nine. Fifty-seven hours a week, plus travel time. What?

He asked me to take the Wonderlic test, a twelve-minute, fifty-question, multiple-choice ordeal to assess a potential hire. I do not test well; I scored a twelve. Alan then reached out his hand to shake mine, and said, "You're hired." I couldn't believe it. This was my first and only interview, I had flunked the test, I had no training in any field, including sales, and I got the job?

When I questioned him about it, he said, "I want you to know that in the history of The Custom Shop, no one has ever scored so low, **but the fact that you have no training doesn't bother me, because you also have no bad work habits**. I can *train* you to be the employee I want you to be."

**"I'm hiring you because of your personality, and that's something you must have, in order to work well with the public.** I can't teach that." I told him that the hours were tough, and I'd have to think about it for a day. I then left the store and met my dad for lunch to ask his advice, as he and I shared a special relationship.

When I was ten years' old, my mom married Joseph E. Gold, the man who had been the lawyer in her divorce action. He was a widower with two children and I became part of a larger family. In a parental shift, he became not only my mom's life partner, but also the father figure who would serve as my role model. He was a successful attorney and well known in grassroots Philadelphia politics.

As the years passed, he was appointed and then re-elected as Judge in Court of Common Pleas 6 and then later appointed President Judge of Common Pleas in Philadelphia.

Prior to moving into the family home, I had spent my earliest years in a Montessori boarding school, followed by a shared-custody agreement that was both scary and lonely; my biological father had removed himself from my life, relinquishing his infrequent custody visits to his new wife, a woman I didn't know. So my new family represented a stability I had not yet experienced—a blessing for me.

I adored my new "Dad". He was a quiet and serious man who seemed to relish my efforts at opening him up to stories and experiences that made him laugh. I could tell him my deepest darkest secrets and knew they were safe with him. He meant the world to me, and I always went to him for emotional support whenever I needed it.

One of my most vivid family memories was my introduction to custom shirts. Each evening, my mom would lay out dad's tie, handkerchief, and a newly pressed shirt—no starch—folded to reveal his monogram - a small **J.E.G.** bordering the cuff. At ten years' old, I remember thinking, "That's so neat!"

Dad would order shirts every two years, and he'd ask me to pick them up at The John Shaw Shirtmakers on Walnut Street. At twelve years' old, I felt very important as I'd enter the foyer and walk down the long hallway that led to this prestigious shop. I knew that our family never flaunted wealth; the monogrammed custom shirt seemed to reflect a badge of honor that my father had earned.

As I was now considering a position in a field that I had previously held in so much awe, this *coincidence* was indeed astounding; it seemed that the ten-year-old me was pushing the twenty-three year-old me in a life direction I had not anticipated. I needed the income this job could provide, but with three children under the age of six, the thought of leaving them in a stranger's care for so much of the time was a hard choice to make.

I had been raised in a comfortable home, attended Friends' Select—a private school—spent my summers at camp, and was now facing an employment decision that would take me from my own children for many hours a week. I was *sure* my dad would say, "No child of mine should work that hard. I will help you financially, so you can stay home and take care of my grandchildren." Only he didn't. What he said was, "Go for it, Pumpkin!"

And I did.

At a time when women were not valued as an important part of the workforce, this was a huge shift. Alan Bresnick gave me the chance to break through that notorious glass ceiling and enter a man's industry, and I was on a career path I had never expected. I had stepped into the unknown, and someone I barely knew had opened my world to a new possibility.

**I had now experienced my first lesson in business: the powerful gift of mentoring.** With it came the hope that someday I could pass it forward by giving someone else that same chance.

*** 

Chapter Recap: When an opportunity presents itself, jump in with your mind open to learn, and keep your glass half-full. Stay positive. When you look through the eyes of possibility, you create your own future.

CHAPTER

# The Handshake

By 1966, I was a solid member of the sales team and found that I worked well with my Manager and Assistant Manager. I was frequently asked to close a sale, and month after month I helped our shop achieve its bonus status.

Alan Bresnick was right. I was a quick study for the sales information that had to be memorized as part of The Custom Shop training. I also loved talking to people. I found that I had a knack for sizing up clients and suggesting merchandise that made them feel good about themselves. **I was friendly but not pushy, I established eye contact,** and learned that my natural interest in their stories became a way to remember snippets that I could ask them about when they returned for future purchases.

**I was establishing "my book" of contacts (without even being aware of the process) and I now had a following of people who would ask to work only with me.** I was in daily contact with the city's *movers and shakers;* working with media giants, athletes, political leaders, and CEOs of Philadelphia's most important companies, as well as some from Philadelphia's notorious 'underbelly.' It was exciting to be working with all of them, and I was doing a job I loved. It was a perfect match for someone with so little training.

There's a saying in Yiddish that something is *bashert* when it's destined to be. Just as the *coincidence* occurred that allowed a newspaper to be dropped at my door by mistake, I was about to be presented with another fortuitous opportunity.

Alan Bresnick—who became a friend as well as my mentor—followed my success and felt there was another step I could take that would alter the way women were viewed in the shirt industry. He knew I was still struggling financially and made the call that would establish my career.

"Nancy, how would you like to make more money?" The question was a no-brainer. He suggested that I come to New York for a training session that would teach me how to measure clients and be trained as a shirt designer.

I found a sitter for the children, grabbed my briefcase, purchased my train ticket to New York, and was soon in the private elevator on my way to meet Mortimer Levitt, Founder and President of The Custom Shop national shirtmaking chain, at his office on Fifth Avenue.

As we got off the elevator, Alan said to me, "Nancy, shake my hand." I think I said something clever, like "Huh?" He said, "Do it." I reached for his hand and gave him my normal handshake. He said, "Well done. He'll love you. **You have a firm grip, and that's something Mr. Levitt uses as a first impression.** I noticed it when I hired you, and I just wanted to be sure this handshake was your normal greeting."

I've never forgotten that exchange.

My interview with Mr. Levitt went exceedingly well, and he seemed to be more than pleased by Alan's suggestion that I be considered as a shirt designer. He also said he'd prefer if I took off ten pounds. I was hardly heavy, but it was the 1960s, and women in the work force were still treated differently than men in that regard and could be spoken to that way.

The day went longer than expected and it was arranged that I'd be provided with a hotel room so I could spend a second day there for additional training. I had not prepared for this and when I checked in, all I had was my briefcase and pocketbook. (I ran out to purchase a change of clothes the following day.)

I was so excited by this entry into the corporate world that I never realized it would be open to misinterpretation about my checking into a hotel without luggage. Sometime in the early evening as I was studying my new manual, I got a call from the desk asking if I was open to spending a night with one of their business clients. I was outraged. "You would give my room number to a stranger? How dare you?" He said, "Well, what did you expect? You're traveling alone with no luggage." Until that moment, I had been quite unaware that women were not seen as business people.

I was a woman business traveler at a time when women were still held as homemakers and not respected as part of the business world. It never occurred to me that the road I had taken was so untraveled.

\*\*\*

I returned home the following day, armed with the knowledge that would take my career to its next level. The store manager was instructed to oversee my technique and allow me to measure as many clients as possible, and I was soon doing much of the designing. Clients enjoyed interacting with me and the increased sales allowed our store to achieve bonus status on a regular basis, which also increased my commission check. The synergy in the shop was pleasant, I really liked my manager, and the job was exciting. I was happily enjoying my new title as *Custom Shirt Designer* when I came in one Monday to find that the manager, who had been there for over ten years, had been asked to leave.

A replacement from New York who had a better *look* was already on site, and this abrupt change was shocking to me. I was horrified to witness these firing tactics and could only sit quietly by as my business world was altered. My outgoing manager was required to do a full store inventory that same day, and if he didn't complete it, he was told his final check would be withheld.

Ouch. Is this how it's done? Would I too be thrown away so quickly should someone change their mind about *me*?

No warning was ever given as management felt those leaving might remove merchandise in retaliation. Business decisions are often harsh and I was unprepared for it. This was my first opportunity to witness such an exchange and it was unsettling.

The new manager did have *the look,* but I sensed an air of entitlement from him, and it was unnerving. You can pick your friends, but you can't pick your bosses, and I had no idea what the future would bring. I was committed to just losing myself in the work I generated and the clients who provided my income. My job was too important to place in jeopardy for any personal reason.

Soon after he arrived, the staff from the firm's other location at 1510 Chestnut Street suggested we all get together to share stories and make him feel welcome. The Chestnut Street store was staffed by a manager and a female sales associate whose sales responsibilities were the same as mine, except she wasn't asked to be a designer at that location.

We all got together socially, and it quickly became apparent that the woman from the Chestnut Street store and the new manager at 1704 Walnut Street were destined to become an office romance.

This is never good news.

My new manager soon asked that staff be switched so she could join him at Walnut Street; our store was now operating with one man and two women, while other staffing additions and substitutions were being handled for the Chestnut Street store.

One afternoon, one of my *regulars,* Marty Keenan, came in for shirts and my new manager asked him to work with her, rather than with me. Marty was an icon in the Philadelphia area and his automobile agencies were well known. He was a successful guy, yet he carried himself without ego and always made me feel we were equals. He was one of the first clients I worked with who shored up my self-esteem and I will always be grateful. As this was a commission-based job, I was scared this was about to become an operating practice and suddenly my paycheck was in question. I was told to "go straighten neck ties," and as Marty was unaware of the office politics, the sale was given to the manager's girlfriend. After the client left, I confronted my new boss and expressed my outrage. Almost on cue, he said, "I am your boss, and I won't tolerate your questioning me. You're *fired!* Take your things and leave *now!*"

I was speechless at first, and then I got angry. I remember saying "You didn't *hire* me, and you can't fire me!" He said, "Watch me" and went to the phone to call the personnel department in New York.

Rather than start a scene in the store, I took my personal belongings, found a phone booth nearby, gathered up all my courage, and called the President of The Custom Shop at his Fifth Avenue office.

To this day, I can't believe I actually did that, **but I've always believed that when you want something, you have to go to the person who can make it happen,** and that's what I did. I needed this job to support my family and I wasn't going quietly.

**First impressions are the ones that count,** and my interview with Mr. Levitt in New York had obviously made more of a difference than I had been told—(the strength of my handshake, perhaps?) He heard my story and shared that I was seen as a valued member of the team. He told me to go home and said the personnel manager would be in contact with me.

That night, I got my call and was told that more changes were happening. In another *coincidence* of timing, the manager of the 1510 Chestnut Street had asked to be re-called to New York as he missed his family there. A new manager was about to be installed, and it was decided that I would be a good match for him in this smaller shop. In a surprising turn of events, I would now be assuming the position of Assistant Manager, and would join him there the next morning.

***

The new manager was a nice guy, it was a good match, and I was able to contact some of my clients from the Walnut Street store, including Marty Keenan who had come to symbolize a break-through moment for me. The difference in the salary generated in the larger shop was soon compensated by the new bonus I was able to generate as an Assistant Manager. I was working a fifty-seven-hour week, but I was *still working*. **Sometimes, when a day starts, you just have no idea how it will end.**

The summer vacation schedule had kicked in. The accepted plan was to cover the store manager's vacation with a temporary replacement from New York City who would run the shop during his absence. By this time, we had been breaking sales records at the Chestnut Street store, and the head personnel manager suggested that instead of bringing in a new face for two weeks, I should be given the opportunity to cover the manager's duties until he returned. I was given my own key, and I was now the boss—for two weeks.

Summers are slow in the custom shirt business because all our clients are at their vacation homes. But by the end of the first day, I was already writing significant business. By the end of my second week—based on store figures from coast to coast—we were number two in the country.

On the last day, the manager called me with an unexpected announcement: he would not be returning. He had gone on a religious retreat for his vacation. While there he decided to enter the Priesthood.

*Really?* Was someone *up there* watching over me?

Once again, another *coincidence* allowed me to take a giant step toward establishing my new career. **While fortuitous events may seem to be all about 'coincidence' or luck, sometimes it's also about paying attention and taking action when the gift is placed at your door.** Sometimes it's both.

My figures were so strong that I was asked to remain. I was now installed as the permanent manager for Store #28 at 1510 Chestnut Street; not only the youngest in the history of The Custom Shop, but the first woman in this nationwide company to achieve that position.

\*\*\*

-------------------------------------------------------

**Chapter Recap**: Always come from strength; to break through barriers, make sure you take actions that will engage others about your commitment and drive to succeed.

-------------------------------------------------------

CHAPTER 3

# Making Personal Connections

Now that I had the responsibility of running my own store, I was committed to presenting the sales figures that would assure management that hiring more female managers was in its best interests. I felt responsible to hold this space for *other* women to enter the men's fashion industry, and I was proud to have been chosen to do so.

The Custom Shop had a rigid but brilliant operating formula model. All employees were required to memorize a selling script and maintain every store in exactly the same way. All store windows were displayed identically by using a team that went from city to city and shop to shop, every two weeks.

No matter what city you were in, coast to coast, The Custom Shop had a look that was clearly identifiable. **The concept I now know as *branding*, I learned about as part of the company's operating practices.** They also had a powerful sales format, and for someone who had not completed college, this training was an extraordinary gift for which I will always be grateful.

I loved being the boss. I was given the opportunity to interview another sales person for my small shop, and I offered the position to a pretty young woman who had a friendly and confident personality. Just as my mentor Alan Bresnick had pointed out, she had the important qualities necessary for this sales position and I knew I could teach her what she needed to know. The shop had now become a two-woman operation and crashing through this glass ceiling gave us purpose. Our shop was always full of energy, the mood was inviting, and some of the city's highest profile people were happy to find such a warm place to just drop in and wind down.

Tom Snyder, a leading TV host in Philadelphia before moving to Los Angeles, became a friend. He would stop by regularly, as did my 'underbelly' clients who always treated me with the utmost respect. They would bring me flowers and showed up just like regular guys ordering shirts; and Sid Mark, the radio *phenom* who aligned himself with Frank Sinatra by playing only his music on his nightly shows, became my radio buddy. He knew I worked until 9:00 p.m. on Wednesday nights, and during my years at this Custom Shop location he would play the song *Nancy with the Laughing Face* and dedicate it to me on air, every Wednesday night.

Twenty years later, I was at The Elan Club, an upscale bar and restaurant that once shared a location at The Warwick Hotel in Center City, Philadelphia. Sid Mark was booked as the Celebrity DJ and I walked over to his turntable to re-introduce myself after so many years.

He looked up at me and said, "Of course I remember you, and look at this!" He shared that the song he had just prepped to play was *Nancy with the Laughing Face*—another coincidence of timing?

Long ago, I stopped questioning these life moments.

For many years, I seemed to be on every party invite list. My clients loved introducing me as their shirtmaker, and while I was making just one hundred and fifty dollars a week during the startup years, I was held as something of a celebrity because of the panache of the profession.

There's something about an artist, in any form, that encourages people to interact with them. Probably my most bizarre story followed the showing of the movie *Alfie*. Michael Caine was in Philadelphia, appearing on the Mike Douglas show. His agent came in for shirts and during the exchange of conversation, he asked if I could get together with them as he thought

Michael would enjoy my company. I still remember having to decline because I couldn't get a babysitter! This fun evening never happened, but the job definitely had perks.

***

While I've always been fairly private about sharing the names of my clients, some had a more profound effect on my life than others.

In the late 1960s, I met Lewis Katz, a young lawyer who had just moved into a law office at 15<sup>th</sup> and Locust. I write this now with a deep sense of sadness as the friendship we had maintained along the years came to an end on May 31<sup>st</sup>, 2014 when his charter plane crashed at take-off, killing all aboard.

Lewis Katz was the son of a single parent as his father died when he was a year old. He was raised by his mother with little to no money and with a fierce drive to succeed.

While his life direction appeared to include the law degree he achieved while on scholarship, he quickly noted that he was not cut out for it. By the time he passed away he had become a billionaire media mogul, a brilliant businessman, and a philanthropist who had donated millions to the Dickinson School of Law as well as a twenty-five-million-dollar commitment to Temple University for their School of Medicine.

Some people use their money to define themselves; Lewis used his money to help and define others. As a poor kid, he knew the struggle of those who shared his plight, and he had the capacity to share himself with everyone from the President of the United States Bill Clinton, to the friends he kept from his earlier years. I was blessed to be included in that circle.

The list of his accomplishments is too long for me to capture here, but the point of this story is to honor a dear friend who never forgot his roots or those dear to him.

Lewis was tall and lanky, and while he was a good looking guy, it was his humor that brightened my days. He could nail a Bill Cosby impersonation better than anyone else I knew. It's no wonder he and Bill Cosby became close friends in their adult years, although given Lewis's ethics, Cosby's subsequent fall from grace would have mortified him had he been present to witness it.

My shop became a regular stop for him in the late 1960s, and while it broke every Custom Shop rule, we'd share a corn beef sandwich right there on my selling table while he would make me giggle at his silly humor.

One day he came by with a red wool coat he had purchased as a Hanukah gift for his wife Margie. For all the pride he felt about this purchase, it could have been chinchilla. He said the color was just perfect for her, and he couldn't wait to see her face when she opened the gift he had so lovingly selected. Of all the gifts he gave her over the many years they shared a life together, I don't think any of them matched the importance of the red coat.

What follows next is the story about **paying it forward.**

Lewis had the capacity to make everyone he was with seem like they were the most important people in his life and that they mattered. Our history together spanned over forty-five years and included many interactions, but the one I forgot (that only *he* remembered) is the one that opened the doors to my making shirts for his friend George Steinbrenner.

Having amassed a small fortune when he sold a parking lot company called Kinney Systems, Lewis found himself investing in several sports teams, among them The New York Yankees. He set up office meetings where I would come to New York for custom shirt fittings with several of the Yankee partners and many years later, when I had opened my own company on Walnut Street, he delivered George Steinbrenner to my studio.

Steinbrenner was the principal owner and managing partner of The New York Yankees and he was everything you ever read or heard about. He was brash and appeared to be almost rude in his demeanor, but underneath all that, his personality was one that reminded me of my dad's. I had spent a lifetime knowing how to shift that behavior into a more appealing one and that's exactly what I did.

By the time I had finished measuring him, George had taken off his World Series Ring, took my hand and then placed it on my finger—Wow. When it was time to leave, I hugged Lewis as I always did and George looked at me as though he had been ignored. (At least that was my take on it.) I smiled at him and then gave him a big bear hug also. As they were leaving, Lewis mouthed the words, "I can't believe you did that!" He then grinned at me, as only Lewis could do, and I knew that he had actually enjoyed playing a role in this special introduction.

We met for lunch one day, and I said to him, "Why are you so kind to me?" You're such a big shot, and I'm just a little shot, hardly worth your time." His answer stunned me. "Do you remember when we used to hang out at that little shop on Chestnut Street and talk about how we thought our lives would evolve? You gave me a referral at one of our corn-beef lunches and it became the first fee I had ever earned on my own."

I had not even remembered doing it, yet *he* never forgot it: Lewis Katz—Irreplaceable. Iconic. Larger than life.—too special to ever forget.

The moral of this story is that you never know who you will meet on the road of life, and that **everything you do for others comes back to you in some form**.

In his commencement speech to Temple's graduating class, just weeks before the plane crash, Lewis recalled a quote by UCLA basketball coach John Wooden that became the touchstone for his life. "You can't live a perfect day without doing something for someone who will never be able to repay you."

Every day, in every way, Lewis Katz helped *someone,* and several of his core beliefs are presented here as a reminder that when you hold strong beliefs, you can accomplish whatever goals you set out for yourself.

- **Success isn't about material things; it's about spending time with friends and family, and making time to have fun**
- **You need two things to succeed: Patience and Grit**
- **If you don't believe in yourself, nobody else will**

- **Study the behavior of those you admire**
- **Live with integrity and a sense of humor**

Lewis Katz, you got your job done. RIP dear friend.

***

---

<u>**Chapter Recap**</u>**: Everyone has the ability to help others, and a hand-UP is not a hand-OUT. Cherish and honor your connections as they represent the intangible inventory that helps you grow.**

---

CHAPTER

# Doors Open, Doors Close

1966 was the year I was fully on my own at the little shop at 1510 Chestnut Street. Business was solid, and people waited at the selling table until we could get to them. One of these clients was a good looking and seemingly successful man who would soon become Husband #2. We married in 1968, and my family grew by one more child when his toddler son came into my life.

Just after our wedding, he lost his job and couldn't seem to find another that matched his expectations. **Why is it that some people decline the jobs they're offered, because they don't match the income they made previously?** Excelling at a new job will eventually pay the dividends you seek if you have the drive and patience to achieve your goal—**Why do some people choose *nothing* over something?**

The kids got along well and my job was rewarding, but my husband was challenging. Managing a job and four youngsters was made even harder for me because he was not the provider I had expected him to be, in spite of his very evident charm. (He seemed to find money for leisure activities, but I never really knew where it came from, as he was always working on a "deal" somewhere, and our living expenses were paid from the income I provided.)

My paycheck became a vital part of our monthly budget. While I was becoming resentful, I had also completely fallen in love with his little boy who had become part of our newly blended family. Now, more than ever, my job's stability kept us together.

Everything changed in 1972.

My mentor Alan Bresnick who had hired me, left the company to open one of his own, and a new personnel manager was named as his replacement. The new hire was someone who put a higher value on male management, and as I was the only female manager in this national chain, he wanted me *out* of that position. With no warning, I was told that I was to be replaced by a male manager who had been trained at the Fifth Avenue flagship; I would be expected to serve as Assistant Manager back at the Walnut Street store. As this new manager had already been chosen for the shop and would be arriving in the morning, the switch would be effective *immediately*.

What?

It was explained that I *should* be able to make up most of the difference in my pay, as the Walnut Street store did more business. I was almost speechless, but I remember saying, "Please, don't do this! If I leave management, I forego my monthly bonus, and this is the check that pays my family's mortgage! I can't afford to leave this position and go to the other store." My plea landed badly. It was a take it or leave it offer, and when I said I couldn't financially survive in that position, they said, "Well then, you're *fired*."

Only this time—it was real.

As was the practice, I was asked to complete a full store inventory prior to my leaving. I had more than delivered for this company, yet I was being replaced because I was a woman? I was angry and said "I'll just leave then." I was ready to walk out the door when the man sent to relieve me held up my weekly pay check and said, "If you want to get this, then you'll have to do the inventory. If you want your unemployment benefits, you'll *do* this inventory."

I did what was asked. Only when I got to the bank did I look at the check and noted it had been dated weeks before. This had not been a sudden decision, but I was the last to know about it. I felt completely worthless, and I hadn't experienced that feeling since my first marriage had ended. I now had to go home and tell my husband the news and alert my four children about the change in our lives. I never felt so alone.

The next morning, I awoke with a clarity that gave me power; **I was not going to be a victim.** I decided to channel my rage into more pro-active behavior and take the steps that would right this terrible wrong. I dressed and went to the unemployment office to sign up for my unemployment checks, feeling this would provide the safety net I needed until I could find another job in sales or management.

When you're used to driving your own income, it's *never* a great feeling to be standing in an unemployment line. I was embarrassed and scared. I filled out my papers and was told I'd be getting my first check as soon as the waiting period had passed.

But the check never came.

Instead, I received a formal notice that my claim had been questioned by my previous employer. Because they said I had "quit," they were denying my claim. How do you take *that* on? By taking *them* on! I asked for all the rebuttal forms needed and presented my case with strength and sincerity. I was fighting for my integrity as well as a paycheck, and I couldn't allow a corporation's change of management to diminish my efforts over those many years. As good news, I won my case. I beat a *Goliath* who had tried to stop me—the *David* in me prevailed. Flip side? This was the only job I had ever held, and after seven years of employment, I could not list The Custom Shop on my resume. How would I secure another job if I had no way to explain what I had been doing during that time? The answer came from a surprising contact.

I have always experienced the custom shirt industry in Philadelphia as one that was, and continues to be, a wonderful example of camaraderie. We shared stories, warned other shops about clients who were hard cases so they would not place themselves at risk, and generally held each other as colleagues, rather than competitors.

The John Shaw Company, a shirtmaking company that also shared a Walnut Street location with The Custom Shop, was owned by John (Jack) Shaw, a man who had originally been an illustrator with *Colliers Magazine* but decided to get into the business of custom shirt making. (From our conversations, I was never sure if this life direction was the one he really wanted to follow, but it was the one that established him in a lifestyle that served him well.) He was a great guy, and always ready to share a story (or a martini) with those of us he had a good feeling about, and I was in that inner circle.

When I realized that I had no reference to provide for a job interview, he said, "Use me. Just say you were here as a designer for all that time." Who *does* that? As I look back on it, I find it fascinating that the man who offered my safety net was also my dad's shirtmaker for so many years.

I had never expected such a response, yet I was now supported by the work history that was necessary to secure a new position.

\*\*\*

I needed a job, and I needed it *now*. A *Philadelphia Inquirer* sales ad soon caught my attention. A store in Center City called The Limited was new to our area and this opening happened during its early years, before it became The Limited as we know it today. The store emerged as a concept started by Leslie Wexner, whose parents had operated a woman's clothing store in Ohio.

In 1963, the Wexner's son borrowed some money from the family; along with a small bank loan, he opened his first store. Observing a parent generate an income often leads to an entrepreneurial way of thinking in the child, as my own children would tell you.

By 1969, Leslie Wexner had taken the company public. By 1972, a job opening was offered in this Philadelphia store, and armed with my first resume and a wonderful referral, I was *sure* I'd be chosen for this new position in management. I was not yet beaten back by people saying how hard it was to find a job because The Custom Shop position had happened so easily.

The interviewer loved my resume, but in an unexpected response, I was told I was *over-qualified* and my salary needs could not be matched. How is this possible? I was applying for the job offered and for the pay schedule it presented; how could I be dismissed so easily? I was told "You won't be happy here because your abilities are clearly stronger than those required, and we feel you'll not be motivated to remain with the company."

I remember pleading with them (an embarrassing position to take) that I would be happy and *honored* to work in this new store, and asked that I just be given the chance. The salary was clearly more than the unemployment check I was now receiving—but the job was not offered to me.

This was a sale I could not close.

I returned home to my family to find solace in making beds, doing laundry, shopping for food, and cooking meals. I continued on my new quest to find a job that matched my skills and salary requirements, but good paying jobs for women were hard to find, and during those years any jobs of value were usually held (and filled) by candidates who were men. Women were still seen as homemakers, and the *Man of the House* was meant to be the provider—except in our house.

Every week I visited the unemployment office to sign for my check and present the job searches I had attempted during the previous week. I was embarrassed to be on the dole, but collecting my check provided the safety net we needed. It occurred to me this could be an opportunity to compel my husband to take a more responsible path as the bread-winner of our family.

Now that I was more involved with homemaking, rather than spending so many hours away from my family, the issues of a blended family became more noticeable. My husband adored his son, and while he generously shared in the parenting of all our children—and did an admirable job with that—his emotional attachment was noticeably different when interacting with his own child. In truth, from a financial point of view, the marriage had not been a good idea. I was, however, committed to its success. I had already subjected my own children to a divorce, and now that I was raising my husband's son as well, I felt I could not abandon him. I wondered if having another child might be an opportunity to help define our family unit in a more balanced way. While our marriage wasn't great, I thought that having a child together might encourage my husband to look at family life in a more responsible way. Indeed, the thought of possibly giving birth to a girl was something I had always hoped would happen.

I was already in my early thirties, and while this is young by today's standards, I felt my child-bearing years would soon be over. I also found that after working for seven years and missing so much time with my young children, I was excited about the possibility of being a *stay at home* Mom.

Perhaps this was the perfect timing for a life change.

***

<u>Chapter Recap</u>: **Sometimes when a door closes, it causes you to find another entrance. Stay open to the possibility that change is not bad or good, it's just *change*.**

CHAPTER

# Starting Over (Again)

A year later, my daughter Lisa was born and I felt she was the answer to my prayers. While her birth was challenging, and she was held in ICU for several weeks thereafter, I knew she had a "feisty" gene in her, and would overcome any challenge—and she did. The first year of her life was a year of complete adoration, but not altogether stress-free. Her father truly loved her but was unable to provide for the family. I was never sure if, or when, we'd have enough money to pay for our daily needs. Bill collectors were calling every day, and for someone who had been paying our bills promptly and with integrity during my working years, I found the calls unbearable.

By this time, I was bringing in a small income from cleaning houses and using the money for food but I needed a better life plan.

My buddy Lewis Katz, who had befriended me at The Custom Shop, had remained my friend. He had opened a law firm in the Cherry Hill New Jersey area, and I reached out for his help. He was still practicing law, and he offered to contact every business to whom we owed money. He worked out a payment schedule that was easy to meet, and the calls appeared to stop. I was grateful to Lewis for his efforts on my part when I got a call from a company for a balance due my husband had *promised* me was handled. That call was all I needed to push me over the edge.

How could I remain in this marriage when I could no longer trust my husband? My daughter was thirteen months old and I needed security I could depend on.

Some days later, I noticed a house for rent a block away that if secured, would allow me to keep the kids in the same school and not disrupt that part of their lives. When I answered a second bill collector's call requesting payment, I knew I could not live with this continued threat over me and took the steps that would help facilitate a life change.

\*\*\*

My friend Marlene Uhr, who had also been a single mom prior to her re-marriage, recognized my anguish and offered to lend money for my move. The decision was a heavy one, requiring more courage than I could muster at the time. The stage was set—I just didn't have the motivation yet because the divorce would remove my husband's son from my life, and I now had a baby to consider. All things considered, the thought of putting my older children through a divorce, once again, was unthinkable.

I was stuck.

Several days later, I was at the supermarket and wrote a personal check for our food. When the cashier saw my last name, she flagged the manager and asked me to step aside. Our name and address was on the register, along with a notation that my husband had presented a check of his own that had "bounced." I was told I'd be unable to write checks there and was sent home without the food I had purchased for our weekly needs.

**I often remark that we are all able to receive what I call "messages from the universe"—these are the hints that the path we're taking needs a re-direction.** I've also noted that we often ignore these life interruptions. A life change is not always easy to achieve and sometimes when we continue to dismiss the signs, the message just gets *louder* until we listen.

This was a message I could not ignore—this was my catalyst for change.

\*\*\*

The next morning, I asked my friend Marlene to release the money she had offered. I went to the bank and opened an account under my maiden name, met with the landlord, signed the lease, and arranged for a moving company to get us out while my husband was visiting a college buddy.

I was done.

The marriage was over. Once again, it was time to re-build my life. I now needed to find or create an income stream that would provide for my family, and with a one-year-old baby under my care and a small monthly support check from my sons' father for our three children, the challenge was daunting.

I'm always surprised when people say they can't get a job. **You can always find work doing something, it's just that most people feel some jobs or the income generated is beneath them.** I decided that rather than leaving my baby with someone else, I would use my time at home as a baby sitter for newborns. I started my day when my sons left for school and ended it when the mothers of my newborns picked them up. I had four babies to feed and diaper and I charged fifty dollars a week, per child, for this service. The first year and half was a blur. By the time it was over, I found it hard to have an adult conversation with anyone, but earning two hundred dollars a week, at that time, was a decent salary and it was enough to get our bills paid.

The job ended when one of the toddlers threw his bike into our bay window and cracked it. His mom refused to reimburse me, so I called her ex-husband who was happy to cover the expense. My time as a newborn babysitter had come to an end, but something had to replace it.

\*\*\*

My next job was cleaning apartments for bachelors.

The idea came from noticing a growing trend towards a single lifestyle and **when you want to make money, find a need and fill it.** I put an ad in the local paper and advertised my cleaning service, and before I knew it, I had five clients, one for each day. I charged five dollars an hour, and my rules included leaving a key under the mat, my money on the table, and they were never allowed to come home while I was there. (I think the last rule was simply because I was embarrassed by having to do this menial work.)

One day, I had just unloaded my cleaning supplies when I heard a key in the door. The man who stood there before me was not my client, and he had a pretty woman with him. When I questioned why he was there, he said his friend gave him the key so he could use the apartment for the afternoon. He then said, "When are you *leaving?*" I immediately responded, "How about *now?*"

I packed my supplies, took the pay my client had left for me and quickly shut the door behind me. That night, my client called and said, "When are you coming back to finish the work?" I said, "I'll be back next week on your regular day. You booked my day, and I was there. There will be no *do-over* and if you want me to continue, you can't ever embarrass me like that again!"

**Time is money, and sometimes when you're working for people who make more than you do, they think their time is more valuable than yours.**

**Don't allow that.**

I was standing up for myself and my needs, and it felt good to express myself in such a powerful way. I got an apology, he continued to be my *Tuesday* bachelor, and I never got another unexpected visit.

I continued this schedule while also looking for a permanent position that would generate a better income. Once again, *The Philadelphia Inquirer's* want ads produced the perfect opportunity

***

In the 1970s, a company called NutriSystem, based in the Philadelphia area, developed a liquid protein that was seen to be a dieting breakthrough. A chain of weight loss centers was opened—some privately held by the parent company—with many more opening as franchises. One of the franchises in the New Jersey area was looking for a sales person who could work a lead.

I applied for the position. The job split was 9 a.m. to noon with an afternoon break and then 3 p.m. to 6 p.m. to complete the day. This was perfect for me, because the hours allowed me to work around my family's schedule. I presented well and landed the job easily.

There was a training program that included learning the manual that explained the company's vision, as well as a presentation on enrollment techniques that would help dieters achieve their desired goals. Liquid protein seemed like a magic potion, and I was trained to enroll their interest by signing them to a contract that covered their weight loss program. The contract would include their supplement, coaching, and weight management support that would chart their progress over a selected period.

Once again, my skills allowed me to excel, and I was able to generate large weekly paychecks because my training at The Custom Shop provided the perfect finishing school for sales training.

Even then, I noted this simple fact: **If you have good people skills and a strong sales personality,** *you can sell anything*; shirts, ties, cufflinks, liquid protein, contract sales, automobiles—what's the difference?

(In fact, this reminds me of my former Custom Shop client who owned a Rolls Royce agency. He always complimented me on my selling technique and offered me a job at his agency every time he purchased shirts. I always turned him down because I held The Custom Shop as my career.)

I watched the NutriSystem office receipts grow and after a successful year, the partners purchased matching Lincoln Continentals. The partners then decided that if one office was a great idea, having *two* locations would be even more lucrative and so they over-extended.

**At the time, I knew nothing about entrepreneurial behavior, but I noted they were spending profits too quickly and moving too fast.** When the second office opened, I was called into a meeting and told my schedule and location would be changed. I was their top sales person, and they wanted my skills in the *new* office, farther away. I was again being moved at the whim of the company, but this time my life as a single parent did not allow me to comply. I had a little one at home in addition to my young boys and this schedule would be impossible for me. I told them I could not accept that move as it was not the position for which I had been hired.

And for the *third* time in my working life, I heard the words, "Well then, you're fired!"

Once again, I found myself at the unemployment office, and looking for another job that would provide an income for my family. I was grateful for the unemployment checks, yet even those did not touch my financial needs as a single parent.

\*\*\*

By this time, my husband and I had divorced, and gaining child support during those early years was a nightmare.

If you were a woman who walked that path, the money was hard to get if the ex-spouse had limited income or chose not to comply due to anger or resentment. I was able to get "milk money" at school through government assistance, but the only money I was receiving for support came from a small check from my first husband, and it was barely enough to cover even the boys' basic needs. I was now in *crash and burn* mode. With no support money coming from my baby's father, and my unemployment benefits ending, I was now pressed to apply for welfare payments.

*Welfare*!—Me?

I was embarrassed and wounded, and my personal pride prevented me from going to my parents for help. I made an appointment for the welfare interview and counted the days until I could get on a program that would offer some financial relief. The stress was crippling, and as the day approached, I noticed a small blister forming on my lip that was sending waves of pain that made my eyes water. By the day of my appointment, I had a fully blown fever blister that was festering in a way that matched the emotional pain I could not heal. As I sat in the room, surrounded by a sea of scared and needy people, I felt completely defeated.

My interview was a disaster.

It appeared that the four-hundred-dollar monthly support check I was receiving for my three sons was deemed to put me over the limit for the additional assistance I needed. How could this be? I was receiving no money at all for my daughter—how could I be denied? I was, however, asked to take a picture for my welfare card. The fever blister on my mouth was hard to miss; it was a picture that captured the look of a person who had hit bottom. I left the office with the ID in hand that allowed me to share in the food stamp program, and a driving need to heal the emotional and financial pain that I was experiencing.

I still have this picture.

**I keep it to remind me that the bottom is only a temporary resting place, and when life gets tough, it's simply an opportunity to find a new future.**

It also keeps me humble. When my career had started, my dad had said, "Go for it, Pumpkin,", and now my only question was, "Go *Where?*" Without labeling it, I thought: "**When you want something, put it out there.**"—and my own version of *networking* soon evolved.

A friend of mine was close with someone who was bringing in merchandise from China and had fully stocked a store location at the Pennsauken Mart in South Jersey, a place that served people with limited incomes. He was looking for a store manager he could trust, as it was a cash-driven operation. My friend knew of my integrity and drive and felt I was a match for his buddy's new business venture. I was soon offered the opportunity for a night/weekend job that included two ten-hour days, a Thursday to Sunday schedule, and a weekly salary of three hundred dollars' cash to run it.

Since leaving The Custom Shop, this was the most money I had ever made. For the first time I felt secure about money. The feeling was wonderful, but the hours were long and the work environment was harsh. I still remember the smells of cotton candy and pizza that greeted me nightly, and the constant call of the Spanish words "Mira, Mira" was impossible to ignore.

The store was generating a decent income for its owner, but his intention to roll this out as a multi-store concept was too challenging for him. He knew he could trust me to manage the store and be honorable about the income it produced, but he didn't think he could replicate it, as staffing for additional stores would be too difficult. **It was an experimental idea that had no legs,** and he decided to close it down.

My income stream was now gone.

***

During our closing conversation, I shared an idea with the owner that was gaining momentum. In the 1970s, it seemed like everyone was single— something I'd noticed in my house-cleaning for bachelor's period—and match-making companies were just becoming popular. People were seeking places to meet in an unthreatening way, and Singles' activities were being run at churches and synagogues.

As a newly single woman, I was also looking for a social connection.

I found myself attracted to The Unitarian Church which was running a weekly meeting that offered Singles a chance to meet in small groups and share their experiences. It was not the *bar scene* that everyone railed against, but a comfortable way to exchange ideas and meet like-minded people who were looking to connect more comfortably.

After attending several sessions, I felt it was a wonderful concept to replicate, and I talked more about it with my mart store employer. Without understanding the terminology at the time, I found I had actually *enrolled* him into the idea of a partnership to bring this idea forward. He said he'd get back to me about arranging a meeting that would hammer out a partnership agreement, develop a plan, and work out an operating schedule. He said he'd be going to the Orient for six weeks, and when he returned we could flesh out the idea I had presented to him.

**Sometimes an easy idea is just that. Some people dissect and re-create in a way that beats it to death.**

I was already on overload by his pep talk, and I just wanted to get into action. I was energized by this new social direction, and found myself quickly creating a concept that would match the needs of this newly single lifestyle. *Stella got her groove back!* (This was the theme of a movie some years ago and when this feeling happens, it provides the space for a new beginning.)

I was now energized, and I got busy shaping the format that could provide another path toward independence. While this would be my first experience as a *Start-up* business, it was simply addressing a need that reflected a sign of the times.

***

**Chapter Recap: In any business climate, find a *trend* and hop on it.**

6

# Standing in the Middle

I've always been a believer in having a financial safety net, and when I started the Mart job, I made sure I put some savings away. It wasn't a big number, but it was enough to get a designated phone number and an answering machine that would become "the office" for this emerging business concept.

There were so many other options and places for people to meet, that I named the entity The Other Place for Singles. Since the group with the most name recognition was The Unitarian Church, we were The Other Place—TOP. I located a meeting place called The Marion House in Cherry Hill, New Jersey that I was able to rent for one night per a week at a nominal fee. It was already equipped with chairs and had a space that could easily be turned into a reception area. I decided that the cover charge would be four dollars for the night, to match the going rate of the other places I had attended. I wanted to provide a similar, and hopefully even better, experience for the same fee.

I had a small budget reserved for soda, punch, pretzels, celery and carrot sticks, plus mini bagels (which I hand cut) and the lox and cream cheese spread that I also mixed by hand the night before. It became a trademark part of the menu and a pretty great deal for just four dollars.

As part of the marketing effort, I placed an opening announcement on supermarket bulletin boards in the area, and asked every friend I had to put the word out to every *single* person they knew. With a target number of eighty people, I knew there would be enough to cover expenses, and still provide a small income for the work it generated. **This *start-up* was now ready to go** (although at the time, this phrase was hardly as well-known as it is today.)

When my mart employer returned six weeks later, he opened his mail to find an invitation to the opening event. Moving fast has since become one of my operating principles, and this was my first experience of doing so.

**This was my maiden *entrepreneurial* venture**, but I wasn't aware of it *as a concept,* at that time.

During the run of its existence, TOP events (The Other Place) were held in several locations, and the format was always the same. Our discussion nights were held weekly, consisting of eight to ten groups, with eight to ten people in each group, as well as a group leader who would be the facilitator. By this time, I had a group of friends who joined me in the effort by volunteering to be group leaders, and every weekend we would decide what the Tuesday night topic of discussion would be.

Group leaders were also single, and were given a free pass for the evening.

The discussions served as the ice-breakers that encouraged the group to share their thoughts and experiences about single life, but it was really about creating an opportunity to meet "the one" in a non-threatening way. I held the concept as though I was planning a house party, and the numbers needed were small enough that I felt we could fill the chairs. I was operating on adrenalin.

From the first night it opened, it was an immediate success. **It never occurred to me that it could fail.**

The weeks sped by, and I decided to add what I called "a special interest group" in addition to the discussion groups. Each week, I would call in someone who would offer those who signed up the chance to discuss a topic of interest. We had psychics, authors of self-help books, Rolfing experts, accountants, lawyers, financial planners, feng shui designers, marketing experts—anyone I could think of that might put a different "spin" on a night out for Singles. By this time, I had met someone at one of my own events who was interested in being part of this fun evening and we became the team who managed the night's activities.

My oldest son Steve was a teenager at the time, a terrific dancer, and I added another group for those who wanted to learn the newest disco steps. I paid him fifty dollars a night out of the proceeds, and he became a permanent member of our "staff." (It was also his first job, and while it negated my needing to give him allowance money, it also became a *teaching moment* by providing him with an income he generated himself.)

I then added monthly dances, and even secured several clubs which were willing to rent their space, as I always chose off-nights when the clubs were not in use.

The Other Place was really fun, and it was creating a buzz. *Philadelphia Magazine* had a segment called *People To Watch* which was done every year, and it showcased the number of people reflected by the year it represented. My buddy and I were chosen as part of the *76* people to watch in 1976. A photo shoot was set up, a picture was selected to represent our inclusion in this list, but at the last minute, our names were pulled. We represented *two* people, and therefore represented *77* people for their 1976 list. His interest soon ebbed, as he met a friend of mine at one of our weekly evenings, and I continued running the group on my own.

On the plus side, The Other Place made a huge difference in the lives of hundreds of people. Many people met there, and some later married. In fact, two of my friends to this day, Eileen (who I have always lovingly referred to as Reds) and her husband Mark Barbush met there, and Reds showed up at one of the evening session in her wedding dress. Talk about marketing!

And they weren't the only ones, as I too met the man I would later marry. My soon-to-be husband was a racquetball player and taught me the game.

It was so much fun, that I added a *Singles Racquetball Night* to the schedule. Looking back on it now, I realize even more how much this entrepreneurial idea was a life-changer for many.

**I continued running TOP for several more years, and it was during this time, that I recognized the concept of *Standing in The Middle* when managing money.**

When you generate an income yourself, money comes in—and money goes out. I was able to see that if I just *stood in the middle* of this money stream, I could also use it until the day I had to send it along to pay my bills. I always seemed to have a cash float, and I always paid my bills, so the practice became a perk of business ownership that I had never expected.

I also set up a practice to *make sure* those bills would be paid by writing the checks out right away and leaving them in an envelope on my desk. **I would place the due date where the stamp would go,** so I knew they'd go out on time.

I was making money, but also spending it, as I was now running a business. I needed money for food, invitations, staff and/or clean-up crew, office supplies, rental fees, office support and marketing. I started creating newspaper ads in some of the small local papers, and before long, I had become proficient at doing so.

I later became friendly with the owner of one of these small newspapers, a *Singles* paper that was filled with places to go and things to do. To make more money, I sold and wrote ads for others, including some of the clubs I used for our events.

This was the beginning of my introduction to the strength of *Marketing,* and this early entry served me well, as I later became even more and more entrepreneurial in my marketing interests.

The Other Place was a name and not a place, and as time passed, I found I needed to keep moving it to alternate locations whenever the space was required for other events. I moved it to a few private clubs, one of which was Ramblewood Country Club in Marlton, New Jersey.

The facility was wonderful, and the owners were very gracious. At one of the events, I was introduced to a friend of the owner who had a private club in Center City, Philadelphia, complete with meeting rooms and an indoor swimming pool. This was a chance to have a location in the city; I was excited about this new opportunity. It was called Cobblestones, and when I visited the facility, I knew it was a match.

Cobblestones members who were single were allowed to join us at no fee, as an added perk for their membership, and TOP visitors were allowed to use the pool. The Cobblestones location was ideal, and I arranged with the parking lot under the building to allow parking at a nominal fee. There was also a restaurant on the lower floor for those who chose to meet for more socializing after the groups ended. TOP had an on-going presence there for some time until a transition occurred when the name was changed from Cobblestones to The Society Hill Club.

One night, one of our TOP people went to the restaurant after the event and purchased a meal. She left without paying, and I was pressed to cover it.

Every week for several years, I had charged only a four-dollar fee for an evening's entertainment, a chance to make a significant social connection, a one-dollar parking fee for the night, free pool access, free dance lessons, free beverage and food, and someone now expected me to cover their dinner expense? I was livid.

Perhaps the shift to The Society Hill Club was a signal that the future held real change, and perhaps I was just tired of this mode of generating; but in the moment I paid the uncalled-for food bill, I knew it was done and TOP had run its course.

This was a "message from the universe" I felt compelled to heed.

I drove home to New Jersey, and changed the tape on the answering machine— "Hello, this is Nancy Gold with an important message. After many years of providing a meaningful service, The Other Place for Singles is now *closed*. Thank you for your support."

**The smallest gesture can be the catalyst for a life or career change, and sometimes the best way to deal with this insight is with speed and purpose.**

I was once again on my own, and I now wanted to find (or create) what I hoped would be a *real* job. My time of *standing in the middle* was over.

Now what?

\*\*\*

Chapter Recap: Every action you take creates the next teaching moment. Being pro-active allows you to seize that moment when it's good and to walk away when it no longer serves you. You are only one thought away from your next success.

CHAPTER

# Moonlighting

During the years TOP existed, I had most of my days free. I had maintained my friendship with shirtmaker John (Jack) Shaw, and it occurred to me that by using my free hours pro-actively, he and I could use the connection to our mutual benefit. I had begun a client list while at The Custom Shop, which many in sales would now refer to as "their book." As someone who chose sales as a career, I've already noted that when you are good at sales, you can sell *anything*, and **when you're in sales, your book is sacred. Your book is the storefront for your business,** and you can take it anywhere you want to go. **In fact, your *book* is so valuable, that many businesses will hire you, based on its strength.**

Now that I had a client list, all I needed was someone to make the shirts for me. In today's business world we'd be talking about finding a *contractor* as the supplier. (At the time, it was just a need that I had to fill.) I approached Jack and asked if he'd be willing to charge me a per-shirt price for a finished garment, and I would find a company to make a label identifying it as my own custom shirt line.

It was a win-win for us both, as I was generating new business for him and providing an income for myself. Without any knowledge of the concept of *Private Labeling*, that's exactly what had occurred.

My company was now *Designed by Nancy* (not terribly clever, but it was my rainmaker) and every shirt success I achieved was rooted in that initial jump-start. I found I had become fearless in my quest to secure new clients, and when I met people socially who knew I was a custom shirtmaker, the panache led to a sale, and after every sale, I asked for my next lead.

One of my best supporters was Pepe Levin, who was known as "The Silver King," a South Jersey icon who bought and sold silver. He melted it down and re-sold it at an enormous profit, an illegal practice that classified him as one of the largest silver dealers in the country; his lawyers kept him from being jailed for this offense, but several years later, he was eventually imprisoned for tax evasion. (For more on Pepe Levin, go to Chapter Nine.)

I had heard of his reputation, and in my quest to raise money for my family's needs, I wanted him to buy silver proof sets I still owned. He thought I was "spunky" to track him down, and he made time for our meeting. I met him one afternoon at his legitimate business called Rochester Formals on Route 38 in Camden, New Jersey, and when I entered his office there was a ticker tape running (with silver prices, I assume.) He had a real Damon Runyon type of presence—gruff, but in a likeable way.

My dad (whom I adored) had a similar affect, and as I knew how to charm someone who came off in such a rough manner, I was comfortable with our exchange. He bought my silver coins, and when he learned I was a single parent doing outside sales for custom shirts to earn money for my family, he offered to help me find new contacts.

This interaction became a large part of the additional income I generated during that time. Pepe knew a fair number of celebrities, and while he never ordered custom shirts for himself, he sent a car to pick me up at my home, delivered me to the client he wanted me to work with, and then paid for any shirts they ordered.

He always tried to *hit* on me, and I think the main reason we remained friends is that I always turned him down. After a while, it became a strange *dance* to be with him, as on some weekends, he'd pick me up and take me to a winery owned by a friend of his and buy me a case of wine, or find a quaint place for a country lunch. It was reported that he was buying seven hundred and fifty thousand dollars' worth of silver certificates a week, and given that activity, I assumed that someone in his line of work had few people he could trust. He just *liked* me, and he said I was always a happy part of his day. He and I worked together for some time, and while he was often referred to as a member of "The Jewish Mafia," he was just an unpolished guy, with a big heart—at least with me.

I still had youngsters at home, and this type of selling allowed me to set appointments around their needs which still included picking them up from after school activities, and handling the daily chores of a homemaker. This was my entry into *multi-tasking*, but it wasn't expressed that way then— it was just doing what needed to be done.

The John Shaw Company soon found they needed a swing person to cover Jack's clients when the staff went on vacation, and with several years as a designer behind me, that swing person became me. I made a day's pay that included a small commission, and between my side business and my part-time job as a designer, I had enough to handle the needs of my young family.

In the late 70s, the country was experiencing a financial crisis, but it seemed to only hit those with moderate means. It was a time when the rich did have money and were happy to spend it. Interest rates on CD's were paying double-digits, and custom shirt sales were still strong. Business attire required a shirt and tie, and people with money loved the panache of custom shirts that included their signature monogram.

We were slammed with business.

At first, I was just called in as needed, but as the need increased I was soon working four afternoons a week. I loved being there. The product was superb, Jack was a real gentlemen and very kind to his employees. There were days that he would buy us all lunch, and when we weren't selling he would entertain us with stories about his early days as an illustrator at *Colliers Magazine.*

It was an exciting place to work, since his client list included many from his personal social strata, and they all valued having a woman's point of view about their purchases. I felt no pressure while there; I was respected as a designer and a peer even though my salary was only limited to my commissions.

It was during my days moonlighting as a designer at Shaw's, that I noticed an empty display case at the back of the store just begging to be filled with *something*.

**As a business practice, when you're paying rent, every square inch should be generating an income or providing support for your business.** Rents are expensive and must generate a strong return on that dollar. **When some of that space is not being used, you're not only paying for empty space, you're losing an opportunity for additional income.**

Jack had no interest in filling the display case, so I asked if he would consider allowing me to use it to sell men's gold jewelry. My friend Mark Lichterman had a store on Sansom Street's "Jeweler's Row" in Center City, and he offered to front me some pieces on consignment. **He trusted me to be a person of integrity**, and had no problem providing inventory for this display case.

I cleaned up the case, polished the glass, printed up small business cards which I left on the counter, and paid Jack one hundred dollars a month for the use of his space and address. I called this new business *The Little Gold Shoppe* where I sold solid gold jewelry to the men who were already there to buy their shirts.

**Today, using a small space in another's location is called a "kiosk"**— Was I ahead of my time?

Although I was still selling shirts with my private label, I now had a *business,* so I was at the Walnut Street shop every day. When I wasn't selling jewelry, I was getting a commission on my sales while at the store, and now used this opportunity to watch how Jack made sales, as well as how repairs were handled.

In the custom business, there can sometimes be instances where an operator makes a sewing error, or a salesperson misses a measurement. A six-pound gain or loss could change a collar size significantly (as much as a quarter of an inch.) Men lose weight a great deal faster than women, so a shift in the original measurements was commonplace when shirt delivery took eight weeks, at that time.

When this happened, Jack always offered a correction, but did so without being aware there was an irritating edge to his voice. This was a wake-up call for me.

Why give a free repair and then lose a client because he was now too put-off to return? I decided that if this ever happened to me, I would be as gracious as possible, and tell the client I would be happy to rectify it at no charge. **A service business sells *service*, and the way to do that is to not make a client wrong.**

These are the stories that help grow your reputation. As evidence of that, years later *The Nordstrom Way* (1995) first documented in a best-selling book the admirable business practice of customer service that had become synonymous with the Nordstrom name.

**Positive PR is your best advertisement. Keeping a client is far more important than being "right," and should you wish to maintain a long-standing relationship with him, it's a small price to pay. Remember: your clients have friends, and referrals are the life blood for any business.**

On the flip side, it may also be valuable to consider the 90/10 rule, which is sometimes harder to implement. Many years ago, before the thought of opening my own company was even a possibility, I read a business story that explored the concept that 90 percent of business stress comes from 10 percent of the client list. It was one of those articles that stuck, and I never forgot it. I soon found examples of why this article had merit when I opened my own company.

Sometimes, you just *know* that the client who questions your expertise may be the one person you'd prefer not to engage. I've had clients who have told me stories about how they've treated *other* providers in a hostile fashion in order to get what they want. Should I then believe I'd be the exception, when their behavior was so disrespectful?

I once declined a sale, and the client said "Do you make so much money that you can afford not to take my business?" I responded, "Not at all. I'd just prefer to work with someone who values me and the service I provide, and I'm afraid that working with you might be costly for me."

Incidentally, I came to notice that **the only time I took questionable clients, was when I was operating from scarcity.**

*Never do that.*

With so many hours devoted to a work schedule, it's important to create an environment that serves you. I have wonderful clients who grace my day and create a pleasant experience for all of us. **It isn't always about how much money you earn, but the path you take to achieve it,** and I have always chosen the path of integrity and respect.

***

---

**Chapter Recap:** Once you're on the entrepreneurial path, every step you take becomes the starting point for your next breakthrough.

---

# The AHA! Moment(s)

I enjoyed being a designer for The John Shaw Company, yet I never understood at the time that a sales career had any *professional* merit. For me, working simply represented what I did to pay the bills and have the money to raise my kids. There was no *gravitas* to it, not like being a Doctor or a Lawyer.

I remember having a discussion with my friend Keesie who had returned to school to earn her MSW. I said, "I could never be motivated to get a degree like that." And she said, "Really? I could never do *sales* the way you do."

**This was the moment I realized that I actually had a *real* career as opposed to simply working at a job.** I had never acknowledged it as such, and perhaps it was time to get more serious about it.

I then got back to selling and designing shirts for someone else's company and **like some insights, it laid there for a while because I took no action.**

It was now June of 1978, a notoriously slow month for custom shirts. All our clients had begun their summer schedules and were away from the city. I was straightening some merchandise when two men entered the shop.

They said they were from out of town and just "window shopping" until they caught up with their group.

We chatted for a bit, and I found out they were brothers who owned a small company in New York State and were visiting Philadelphia for the first time. An hour and a half later, they had each ordered two dozen shirts totaling four thousand dollars, which provided me with just an eighty-dollar commission. Clearly, this sale would not have happened if I hadn't worked with them, and certainly not on a hot summer day!

If the sale had not been so large and the commission so small, I probably would have just written it off to another selling day. But this was my *AHA Moment*, and it was delicious.

As I was sharing the news with the company's cutter and patternmaker, I told him this was the sale that made me think about opening up my own company. Without missing a beat, he said "Can we work together? I've been wanting to get out on my own for years."

This was surprising news, but also unsettling, as it would create a big loss for The John Shaw Company if he left. But he said he had talked to Jack about it previously, and he was now ready to go as Jack had another cutter who could cover his responsibilities. I told him I'd be giving Jack six weeks' notice, and I asked him to do the same.

Since it was the summer, Jack said he didn't need my six-week window, and when I explained that I'd be thinking of a location in South Jersey he wished me well. In a *kamikaze* burst of action, I began shaping the concepts for my own shirtmaking company.

It occurred to me that I had a window of opportunity, given I had just re-married. I put my house up for sale for some "seed" money and we were all soon living in my husband's home. This arrangement provided a safety net for my family, yet financially my husband and I lived separate lives. Even though he owned his own company, I had become an independent provider for my children, and this was the perfect time to take a leap of faith and create a future I could live into.

\*\*\*

Haddonfield, New Jersey called out to me as the perfect location for an upscale business. The town itself was home to many attorneys and proudly offered a vibrant village community that supported its downtown. Driving through Haddonfield, I found myself looking through the shop windows of a property that had no street visibility, but opened onto a courtyard and a parking lot in the back. Mine is a business that doesn't depend primarily on walk-in traffic; it was more important to have vehicular access and easy parking. When I looked inside, I noted that the previous tenants had left shelving and some furniture pieces that could easily be adapted for my own use, and the address had panache: *King's Court*—the perfect spot to grow a new business.

I had created The Other Place as an entity within a six-week window and I was now looking to replicate this same schedule. I had a ten-thousand-dollar profit from the sale of my home and used the money to hire an attorney to draw up a five-year lease with a five-year option, provide enough money to purchase display furniture, two sewing machines, a buttonhole machine and a button sewer, and enough for the security deposits needed for the space. I requested an easy-to-memorize phone number and decided to use my last name of *Gold as* part of the company name, (a name that was short-lived.)

As part of our 'agreement' my cutter would be responsible for the manufacturing, and I would provide the capital, create the space, and handle all the sales. Splitting the profits would be our income. This was a business relationship that was financially unbalanced, yet I needed to make it work in order to go forward with this endeavor. **He had "no skin in the game" as he brought in no start-up money, but he was the manufacturing engine of the company and I could not make the product without him.** I then asked him how little he could make do with until we got the company on solid footing. He said two hundred dollars a week and we shook hands on it. With my three credit cards that totaled fifteen thousand dollars in credit, I soon took a train to the New York City fabric district and spent almost all of it on shirt fabrics.

By July, we were open for business.

The fabrics started arriving and came in so fast that we had bolts of cloth all over the shop, but no clue where to put them. The folded fabrics were easy. I grouped them in colors, and placed them on the shelving the previous tenant had left behind. I left the bolts propped up against the walls because I had no other place to put them, and to my surprise they looked perfect there. I found I had an innate talent for display, and the shop started taking on an eclectic theme that was both comfortable and pleasing to the eye.

I bought a sofa and two chairs; there were no counters or cash register. It was a comfy space that was welcoming, and that was my intention. I needed a large mirror for measuring and it had to be impressive. In my quest to "keep it on the block" and support the other businesses in my town, I went to the antique shop across the courtyard and found the exact mirror that had the presence I had envisioned. The substantial frame was gilded carved wood; the glass was beveled. It was an expensive purchase and became the symbol that reflected the direction I saw for the company.

I draped the windows with wonderful fabrics and put an old sewing machine there for a prop. I positioned some paper patterns that displayed all the parts needed to put a shirt together, and placed the cutting tools nearby. When the windows were done, the effect was both whimsical and elegant, and people started coming in to see what we were doing. I put everything on open view, including the cutting table, so when the cutter was working, you could see it take shape. By the end of the first week, I already had orders on my clipboard.

The week ended with my cutter asking if I could increase his weekly pay to two hundred and fifty dollars. I did so, as it looked like we were already running a business that had great potential, but I wasn't happy about his request. This was 1978, and it was a significant amount of money to pay someone I had considered as a stakeholder in the company.

More business came in on the second week, and when that week ended, my cutter asked for three hundred dollars. Now I was starting to be concerned. **I was taking no money for myself, had all the risk, and yet I was still facing the prospect of splitting profits with him. What was I thinking?** At the end of the third week, his request was for three hundred and fifty dollars, but because he *was* the product engine of the company, I had to agree. By the fourth week, his request was for four hundred dollars as he said he needed more money for his family.

I had sales every day, and even though the sales were covering our expenses, there was nothing left for my own salary. Our financial agreement had become unhinged and I was concerned. At the end of the fifth week, I asked him to add to our bank account as his stake in the company. He said, "I have no money to contribute; I don't want to share profits, I just want to work *for* you."

And that's how the week ended.

Almost on cue, a client I had recently measured stopped in and said he wanted to share an idea with me. He started the conversation by saying, "I hate your company name—it sounds like a jewelry store." **Nothing is more important than choosing a notable company name**, but I hadn't really given it much thought—I had just wanted to get the shop open.

With my last name as Gold, I could see his point and given that I was so recently 'un-partnered', the name change held a great deal of interest for me. I remember saying "if you don't like it, then please give me one you do like." And with that, he threw down a hand drawn logo that showed a crown, placed above a shirt collar, and the name *King's Collar* above them both.

What can you say when someone you don't know well presents you with such a gift? He was so excited by how I had received his suggestion that he said my appreciation was thanks enough for him. I ultimately made him a dozen shirts as my gift for his creativity, but what he gave me was priceless. He not only provided the logo and company name for The King's Collar, but also drew a more feminized crown with the name The Queen's Collar and said that perhaps someday I could use this division to further increase my business. It would take me over thirty years to incorporate it, but he placed that idea in my head as a concept to live into. **No good ideas are ever lost; they just need to be accessed when the timing is right.**

Identifying my company by giving it the right name gave me the credibility I was seeking. To receive this as a gift from a stranger was indeed a business miracle. **I think all businesses have angels, but one has to believe in this possibility**—and I do.

I wish I remembered his name, but I like to think I've honored him by using the name he created and for keeping it viable over so many years. The logo he drew became my formal logo and the one I have been using since that fateful summer of 1978. Somewhere out there a stranger made a difference in shaping my company and I made sure that as the years passed, I was able to pay it forward by helping other businesses in their own marketing and branding efforts.

**Chapter Recap:** Taking an idea to fruition is exciting. Honor the magic moments, yet stay aware of possible breakdowns. A problem can only be solved when it's identified as such.

CHAPTER

# Don't be a Schmuck!

By August, my marriage was over.

It came down so fast, I don't even remember what triggered it. We were married in a small ceremony officiated by Rabbi Fred Neulander, a man who many years later was brought to justice in one of the most widely reported murder trials in recent history. An investigation proved that he had arranged to have his wife killed in order to gain his freedom and be with the woman with whom he had been having an affair.

I only mention his name, because years later, he and my old friend Pepe Levin became racquetball partners, and it was through this connection that Pepe ultimately became his confidante and played a role in helping to bring him down—which I relished. During our friendship, I had encouraged Pepe to become my racquetball partner; later he even wrote to me from Allenwood prison, saying how the game had made his life 'on the inside' easier to bear. He continued to play after his release, and it was during one of their games that Neulander said he wanted to see his wife dead and asked if Pepe could arrange it. Pepe used this conversation in testimony that ultimately put Fred Neulander in prison for his crime.

As I recall our brief marriage, I wondered if somehow our wedding had absorbed the negative aura of the monster who officiated at the solemn occasion. The ending of my 3rd marriage was swift but it was not at all hostile. Both of us were just sad. For two years prior to our wedding, my husband had been my best buddy. Unfortunately, he turned out to be a better friend than he was a husband. His bachelorhood hadn't prepared him for parenting my brood of four children, understandably more challenging than he had expected. Although the marriage ended, the friendship continued and we continued to hold each other with respect.

This would be my last marriage, but while the loss was significant, my attention was now completely focused on building the new company and creating an independent life for myself and my children.

Every August, the custom shirt business starts gearing up for the fall. This includes getting all the fabrics and supplies in place for the new season. At the time, neckwear was a huge part of the inventory I carried, and I was already working with a Philadelphia neckwear manufacturer where I handpicked the silks that harmonized with our shirt fabrics.

I was now into my sixth week of business, and I could see that the business model was working. While there's rarely walk-in interest for this type of custom product, it seemed like the Haddonfield residents and its business community really liked having us there. Access was easy, as you could park at my back entrance, and someone was always coming through our doors. My clipboard had new orders ready for prepping and I was happily looking forward to the fall retail season. The location was perfect, the shop was well received, and while I had sold my house and gone into debt to see my dream fulfilled, the risk was justified. I was a woman business owner at a time when few women had barely thought such a life choice was available to them, and the future looked bright indeed.

As my sixth week of business ended, my cutter asked for an additional four hundred dollars as a "salary advance" to help pay for his children's school uniforms. In 1978, this eight-hundred-dollar outlay (now that he was an employee), including the loan he needed, was almost impossible to fulfill yet **I could not make my product without him.** I'd invested almost all my entire life savings in addition to the credit card debt I had just incurred, so saying *No* didn't appear to be an option. I was compelled to comply. **I realized I had started a company relying on someone else to provide the skills I didn't have,** without realizing the danger this decision included. **Sometimes the obvious is ignored when one is focused on creating a new project.**

**Tunnel vision can be a company's downfall.**

The week ended on this low note, but the following Monday I had an appointment in Philadelphia to select the silks for our new necktie line. I focused on this positive action rather than on the fear and scarcity that my cutter had brought into my life. I now had to work with someone I could no longer trust, yet I had too much at risk to allow anything to stop me— his skills were not yet replaceable and I had to adjust to this unexpected roadblock.

In shaping this new future for myself I knew a lot about what I had to do to get it started, but **I had neglected to plan for *what I didn't know that I didn't know.***

By Monday, I was on my way to the city to work with the tie maker. My cutter had his own key to the shop and usually got there earlier than I did as he liked the quiet of the morning to organize his cutting schedule. I had provided the income he requested and felt secure enough to begin another work week.

I drove from my home to the city, and as I got to the Ben Franklin Bridge, I realized I had left my tie labels on the cutting table and couldn't complete the design day without them. I turned around and headed back to Haddonfield.

When I approached the shop, it was dark.

How was that possible? I entered the shop and immediately called his home, where I got no answer. I cancelled my tie appointment and spent the rest of the day trying to establish contact. I spent three more days trying to reach him, and finally someone answered the phone. I heard a woman's voice saying, "He's left us and we don't know where he went. Please leave us alone."—And then the phone call was disconnected.

\*\*\*

I stared at the phone in disbelief as if the silence signaled the demise of my company. I looked out at the space I had created and knew that the future I had envisioned was now crashing down around me. Six weeks into building the model that was supposed to insure stability in my life, I was now in free fall. My house was gone, along with most of my savings, I had massive credit card debt, and I was running a company that no longer had the support staff to manufacture its product. My 'partner' was simply someone with a dream who had changed his mind, and involved in a family situation at home of which I was unaware.

I had never experienced such terror.

Clearly, my dream had become a nightmare, and the only thing I could do was close down the company and do so with integrity. I noted that I had a five-year lease, with a five-year option, but it included a two-month escrow which could remain with my landlord. As a new business, I had also paid a deposit for my utilities which would cover my shutting them down, and I had four thousand dollars in business on my clipboard, which represented two thousand dollars in deposits that I could refund by using the balance of my savings.

As I was clicking through all these thoughts and contemplating my next steps, I looked up at my beautifully embellished measuring mirror and literally *saw* myself say, "Close down so soon? Don't be a Schmuck!"

I looked in the mirror again and quietly thought, "I'm NOT closing without doing everything I can to save this company!" Literally watching myself make this decision propelled me to get into action. But, where would I start? I was untrained as a cutter and patternmaker—how would I compensate for that?

**It occurred to me that when you don't know how to do something, you need to begin at the end and work backwards. Today this would**

**be called reverse engineering.** I needed to re-create the steps from completion back through its beginning stages, and the most important first step was learning how to make a shirt pattern.

One of the shirt samples still in the shop belonged to a client I had just measured for new ones. He had left a shirt that he wanted us to replicate, and as I laid it out on the cutting table I knew I was about to take a course in *Shirtmaking 101*.

I phoned the kids and said I was going to stay at the shop until I had completed the prep work needed to figure out my next move. The first step was to remove all the stitches from that sample shirt. I found a seam ripper in the workrooms and began the task of taking the shirt apart, stitch by stitch. It took me three days to do this.

When I was done, I put it on the ironing table and ironed it flat. Since I already knew the start-up size, I measured from the edge to the beginning of the sewn lines, and was able to figure out the seam allowances. Once that was done, I compared it to his similarly-sized paper pattern that we use to draft each person's personal pattern. I then worked out the numbers for a mathematical template that would give me the information and ability to draw other patterns in varying sizes.

This first attempt took me forty-five minutes to just figure out the fractions needed for each measurement. I recognized I would have to replicate this process for every new pattern size, but I now knew how to do it. (As time passed, I was able to do that math in forty-five *seconds.)*

My strength was always in sales and designing, but I was now adding another skill that allowed me to enter the field of *patternmaking*. With this insight, I decided I was going to take my best shot and find a way to keep my doors open. I called my clients, told them what had happened, and asked for time to reorganize. I also offered to refund their money. I then reached out to my custom shirt colleagues in New York for a cut and sew resource.

**I have found that asking for help is often the best form of a compliment,** and I was provided with all the contacts I needed to deliver a finished order.

I was still a novice at patternmaking, so I asked my clients to report any errors they experienced in their first early orders. There were many. My friend Lewis Katz once again came to the rescue as I was pulled to address this learning curve. He offered to be part of this "experiment" by trying on those first sample shirts, and by noting the errors, allowed me to make corrections off his personal pattern. My first shirts were horrible, but Lewis ultimately played a large role in helping me carve out my future as a patternmaker. He had the capacity to rise above blame and offered only pro-active comments that allowed me to refine the product. He was my strength at a time when my life seemed to be imploding, and he never wavered in his support. I would not have survived the loss of my cutter/patternmaker if Lewis had not been so patient with me during this critical time.

Since I had the pattern for each client, all I had to do was make corrections to the pattern of a shirt already made and found wanting, and then re-cut it with its new measurements. It took rigorous work to achieve the desired results, the learning curve was very steep, but the concept worked and my clients remained loyal. **Relationship-building is the key ingredient for any successful business venture**, and I have always worked hard to maintain this critical component.

In a surprising response, not one person left me.

As the process continued, I began to excel at the patternmaking craft. Soon I wanted to find a way to keep the shirtmaking operation in-house, in order to achieve quality control. I now had to find a cutter, as well as sewing operators to make the shirts. Finding a cutter happened easily, but I needed a gifted seamstress. I put an ad in the local paper for a machine operator and Adele Stachiotti was one of the respondents. I mention her by name, as hiring her made those early years so special. Sometimes, people have such a presence that you know you want to include them in your life.

Del was that person.

She offered that she had been doing piece work as a part time sewer, and it had become boring for her. She asked what was needed from her, as she wasn't sure she was the right fit. I remember sitting with her, knee to knee, and saying "I have no clue. I was pressed into this by a strange turn of events, and I'm looking to work it out together with someone I like and trust, and I believe you're the one."

This was certainly a strange hiring conversation, but the *trust* part was huge for me, and since I knew *what* to do, I only needed someone who knew *how* to do it. Adele was an excellent seamstress, and we made a wonderful team.

Ironically, I was soon approached by another operator I had known from my days at John Shaw's. He was looking for a sewing position, but I had already given this opportunity to Del and I couldn't go back on my word. I told him that the position was taken, but I gave him the number of another colleague, my best wishes for a successful connection, and followed up with a written referral. **I have always found that it takes no time to do a good deed**, and one should always make that effort whenever possible.

I continued making patterns, and we now had the entire operation under one roof. I began delivering shirts that matched people's expectations, and the business was re-born.

I found out much later that my original 'partner' who ran off, had also left John Shaw without giving any notice. This was clearly his operating behavior and while I should have recognized it at the time, I chose to dismiss it.

**Sometimes, when you have your eye ONLY on the prize, you neglect to recognize obvious warning signals.**

From the day he left, I never heard from him again. It was a slow and tedious process, **but I learned that there's ALWAYS a solution, if you just don't give up.**

\*\*\*

> Chapter Recap: A breakdown can often be a break-through, and it takes patience and faith to achieve that result.

Picture of my first "client" Judge Joseph E.
Gold, as a family snapshot, 1978

# 10

# The Business Plan

The hard part was handled, and I was now over my first (and biggest) hurdle. It was time to get the rest of the staff in place and turn my attention to creating the working model that would best serve the company's future. **When you have a dream, it always comes to you fully finished, yet in real life, you have to create it as it is happening.**

At the start-up, I thought we'd be a two-man operation; my cutter was also a patternmaker and operator. I was the designer/bookkeeper/marketing person, and the ironing and packing would be a chore handed over to a part-time employee. When my cutter disappeared, this model no longer worked and I had to start all over again.

Custom shirts have many moving parts and I was now seeing that I needed more people to handle sales and prep. While I had found an operator to sew shirts, I needed another operator for the detail work that included making the collars and cuffs and running the button and buttonhole machines. I hired Frances Marchese, a local seamstress who worked well with Del, but who did no finishing. I needed someone who could iron and package the orders for delivery and this job was reserved for my son Ira. He became really skilled at it, and took pride in delivering the finished product. I liked the idea of including my children in my work life, as it not only kept them close to me, but also gave them an income that helped to establish their independence.

**I thought it best to hire specific people to do a particular job,** and that way, each person would get proficient at their particular task**, and there would be no in-house fighting about responsibilities.**

Staffing costs had now increased beyond my original expectations, and while I had money flow to cover this new business model, I felt I needed the safety net that a line of credit would provide. One of my neighbors, who had also just begun a business told me that he had a very good meeting at the bank we both used and had no problem having his credit line established. I therefore expected the same positive result.

I had already picked the largest bank in Haddonfield for my account, and as my colleague had already received his own credit line, making this request seemed to be the logical next step for my business start-up. Or so I thought. I had been moving so fast, and handling so many break-downs, that it never occurred to me that my bank wouldn't easily respond to my needs.

When I stopped in to make an appointment, I was asked to see the head teller. The teller then told me I'd have to see an Officer. The Officer then asked me if my *husband* knew I was making this request. When I said I was separated, it was my company, I had no partners, and I didn't need anyone's permission to run or grow it, he said. "This will not be easy to do." As his comment appeared to be an automatic response, it was clear I was already facing some negativity.

Once again, I seemed to be swimming upstream. It was 1978, and very few single women were in management positions, let alone starting companies. He said he doubted if I could get my request filled, but I'd need to talk to the loan department. I made the appointment, and I was told to bring my *Business Plan* with me.

I remember saying, "What's a Business Plan?"

I was *already* in business—did my financial request require such a document? I didn't even know the format for such a plan. I started the company on the strength of an idea, with personal money from my house sale, and three credit cards. I had no advisors, and the concept of a business "coach" was many years away.

I made the appointment anyway, and brought my journal reflecting my start-up sales and a list of the expenses generated by the company. It was a very strong snapshot of a new business that was already covering its financial responsibilities, and I felt confident that my request for a ten-thousand-dollar line of credit would be favorably received.

To my surprise, I was told that I was a bad credit risk for many reasons, and as the banker ticked them off, one by one, I got more agitated by the prevailing attitude.

- **I was reminded that I was viewed as a single woman, and that in itself held risk.**
- **I was a single parent of several children who could be pressed to cover their financial needs.**
- **As I had been married previously, I had no credit history of my own.**
- **Since I had sold my house for start-up capital, I now had no asset there.**
- **I had used the three credit cards for fabric costs, and therefore this added debt was a burden they could not overlook.**
- **I had no personal references who would accept financial responsibility for me.**
- **I had no previous track record of success.**

I was told they could not approve my request, and they suggested I come back again when I had a stronger profile. Why stronger? I didn't *need* the money, I simply *wanted* it. It was to be used as a safety net and since every other (male) business owner I knew had one, I thought I too would be treated in equal measure.

This was a roadblock to be hurtled, not just for me, but to make the point that **women should to be valued and respected in the business world** and I needed to make my mark. It occurred to me that I needed to frame a new type of request to get the result I desired. I'm even more headstrong and determined when I feel I've been discounted in an important way, so I phoned the bank to ask for an appointment with the Vice-President and was granted the time.

As I was already making shirts for some of the bank's biggest clients, I had no problem dropping their names as I was making my presentation. I heard myself say "I've already heard *no* from many sources here at the bank, and my question to you is what action can I take that would have you say *yes* to me?"

He said the question was presented in a way he had never heard before. Twelve years later, this exchange was used in an *Inc. Magazine* article when I was being interviewed as an *Entrepreneur of the Year* Award Winner.

**I added that the best way to insure payment of this debt would be to attach it to my checking account at their bank and have the payments taken automatically when due.** This was the clincher. The idea was well received, and I left the office with the ten-thousand-dollar line I had requested. After a rocky start, I was able to achieve what was then a remarkable break-through.

In an interesting turn of events, the Vice-President later became my client, and we worked together for several years thereafter.

***

---

<u>Chapter Recap</u>: There's always a solution, even when NO is your first answer. When you're starting a company, getting to YES is an entrepreneurial "dance," and once you've received it, the next YES is easier to achieve after you've had the experience of driving that result.

---

# CHAPTER 11

## "You're Fired!"

If you've ever been on the other end of this edict, as I have, then you know how hard it is to hear these words; but as the employer who has to deliver this news, the first one is really tough to do.

When I was an employee, I had not been insubordinate or failing in my work, so these words were especially hard to accept. At that time, I was simply collateral damage due to a management change. But now I was finding I needed to fire someone for insubordination and when you're running a small company, this behavior is simply unforgiveable.

The new cutter I hired had attitude, but I thought this was just personal pride in how she held her skills. She and I shared a "dance," and the steps never changed. As I did every time that she laid out the fabric, I watched her work at the cutting table. I wanted to get a sense of how she did it, so each day I asked her to walk me through the process. She always said it would slow her down and we would get to it at another time.

Interestingly enough, my teenage son Bob who was working with me at the time, had previously offered the following sage advice, "**When running a company, try to make sure you know how to do every step your product requires.**" I knew his coaching had value, but it appeared my cutter was unwilling to take on the role of teacher, and the result was difficult to achieve without her help.

On this particular day, I was especially curious and I said "Let's have that lesson now." I barely got the words out when she said, "I can't teach you this. This has taken me years of training; this is not a job you will ever be able to do because you don't have the skills."

What? (I had already taught myself how to make the patterns she was now using to cut our orders, and cutting was something she couldn't teach me?) I remember saying, "Excuse me?" She then responded, "I don't think you have the ability to learn this."

In an instant, I heard myself say, "Who do you think you're talking to? Everyone is replaceable, and I won't keep an employee who shows me so little respect. Put your tools down, gather your belongings, and get out of my shop! You're fired!"

The words came out, almost without my knowing they were being said; something like having an out of body experience (or perhaps an *out of mouth* experience), because the words just *erupted* from me.

**Note well, that when the day started, this action was not even contemplated.**

I had already survived the loss of my original cutter and patternmaker, and I wasn't about to place myself in a position where my employees had more power than I did. The firing was hostile and my words carried into the workrooms. My sewing operators liked her and when the exchange happened, I was greeted by the shocked look on their faces.

Adele just appeared sad but went back to her sewing. My other operator, Frannie, looked like she had something to say about it. I remember bursting into the workroom and saying, "I won't defend my actions! The door she just walked through is the same door you can use if you can't accept what happened here. If you have something to say, keep it to yourself, and if you can't do that, you can leave by that same door!"

I was greeted by silence.

I then walked back into the showroom, and like the *girlie-girl* I never held myself to be, began to sob. When my cutter left without warning and put my company in peril, I had no time or space for crying; it was clear that I had allowed all the pent-up anger to erupt and it felt good to finally express it.

Adele soon joined me at my desk and said, "I think you need a hug. It's OK. It will all be OK." And just like that, the episode was over.

It appeared that my staff now had a deeper respect for me because I had demanded it. The exchange was never discussed again. The following day, I put an ad in the paper for a new cutter, and by the end of the week we were back in operation as though nothing had happened.

**As the driver of the company, this was my first experience in taking a stand for my operating principles,** and while it was a foreign behavior for me, it was a valuable lesson and it proved to be empowering.

**While it takes courage to remove someone from a job, when you're in the process of defining and shaping a new company, it's critical that you like and trust the team you're leading.**

***

<u>Chapter Recap</u>: Insubordination cannot be tolerated. When you take on the role of a leader, you have to act like one; and nothing creates more respect than standing up for your principles.

# CHAPTER 12

## Enlarging the Footprint

By 1981, the business was solid but my life was still going through personal changes. Although my husband and I had separated soon after our marriage in 1978, we tried once more to make it work. In truth, I always really liked him (and still do.) He was funny and easy to talk to and because he owned a company himself, we had many stories to share. It was a great friendship but we were not meant for marriage and a few years later, the separation was real. While the children and I lived in my husband's home, he owned another nearby and was able to move into it while we figured out how to un-couple in an amicable way.

I had sold my own home when I started the company, and as I had not expected this marriage to end so quickly, I had to find a creative solution that would produce an income for myself and my kids. I had debt to cover while I carved out a new livelihood, and it occurred to me that I could make the transition from married business owner to single business owner, if I could get a two-year financial plan in place.

As we were still legally married, I suggested to my husband that we sign a joint income tax return as a *win-win* situation. He could then claim the five additional exemptions to which he was entitled and give me the amount he would have paid to the IRS as a single person. This would provide the time needed to grow my business by having a financial safety-net in place while doing so. **It was out of the box thinking, and when you're an entrepreneur, you can't survive without it.**

The idea worked. Not all marriages end in *crash and burn*, and this financial agreement gave me the time to get my creative juices flowing again.

I had grown up in Center City, Philadelphia, my roots were there and the City was teeming with additional possibility. I began thinking about this as an idea that might provide increased visibility. I had many clients who lived in New Jersey but had offices in Center City and I thought a small satellite location might widen my footprint.

Sometimes all I needed was to have a thought, and the thought magically became a *thing*—**and that's what happened.**

Karen Kaufman is the daughter of my Aunt's best friend, which makes her seem like family to me, and Karen and her husband Don are colleagues and friends. As a consulting company, Kaufman Partnership worked with corporate executives to enhance their business and personal image. We already shared a vision and worked well together. Karen told me they had a studio apartment at The Warwick Hotel in Center City they were looking to sub-let. They were growing their company, looking at a much larger location, and wondered if I wanted to take over the space.

In yet another coincidence of timing, a new possibility was being presented, and it was enticing. Hmm—a studio location at a toney Center City Hotel—should I? The rent was four hundred dollars a month and this gave me a convenient place to see new clients without a huge rental expense. My son Bob was working in my Haddonfield Shop, and I felt I could float between the two places when appointments were made, while also experiencing the perk of a Center City *pied-a-terre*. It was a no-brainer.

I sub-leased the space, found some comfy furniture, found another great mirror, hung some patterns up on the wall, and it was suddenly transformed into a working studio that served to widen our ever-growing clientele. I turned a small kitchen into a pattern room and I would take my orders there and draw the patterns out on the Formica kitchen counter top. It was quiet and conducive to the concentration I needed to shape this important work product, and it also provided a toney address that my Center City clients could easily locate.

***

One night, after a particularly arduous pattern-making day, I decided to stay over and wandered into the newly opened Elan Super Club, just off the Hotel lobby. I knew it was a membership-only club, and through a chance meeting with the owner, **I found myself doing what I do instinctively, and that's enrolling someone into the possibility of working with me.** I introduced myself as the President of King's Collar Shirtmakers; a company that was an exact match for the demographic they were seeking. I then offered to promote the club in exchange for my clients receiving a free membership. The idea was so well received that I was given a free membership myself. I was pleased by this gesture and reciprocated by making a promotional order for the club's owner, an order that soon provided me with a trade account. **Today this effort would be called *co-marketing*,** but at the time I thought it was simply an idea that could be beneficial to all parties involved.

The Elan drew a crowd of the wealthy and well-connected; the perfect opportunity for me to meet and mix with the City's most influential people. I've been described by one of my clients as "ebullient" by nature, and as my networking skills emerged, this attribute has always served me well. This was the perfect location to test these skills. My connection at Elan became one of the most powerful tools I ever had in growing our company's identity and it came from—yet again—a *chance* meeting that turned into a career-changing event. **As an entrepreneur, you are always selling *yourself*, and in that space, it's important to note that one should lose no opportunity to do so.**

One evening, I stopped at the club and found a seat near the backgammon area. *Happy Hour* was always an active scene, and from my perch I was pleased to enjoy a few moments to wind down from a busy day and perhaps create an opportunity to make new contacts. The seat beside me was taken by an attractive man who nodded a greeting and I smiled back. **Sometimes all you have to do is say "Hello," and that's exactly what I did.** He shared that his name was Mike Murray (D. Michael Murray) and he was a Washington Attorney and Lobbyist, and an active member of the Walter Mondale for President Election Committee who advanced the Candidate's trip to Philadelphia.

As my studio was in the hotel building, he was intrigued by the thought of being measured for custom shirts while there. He made an appointment for the next morning and I offered to deliver the shirts to Washington when they were ready. He was so pleased by this personal service that he arranged for me to see six partners at Patton, Boggs, and Blow, a large and powerful Washington law firm.

Patton Boggs has since evolved as one of the thirty largest law firms in the world after its 2014 merger with the multinational firm of Squire Sanders. **Networking is the life blood of every business**, and meeting Mike Murray took my business to an entirely new level by opening the door to this prestigious firm.

As of 2016—more than thirty-five years later—I continue to have a working relationship with two of my original contacts, Jeff Turner and John Jonas. (Cliff Massa, Mike Murray and others have since moved on.)

My hotel sub-lease was ending, and as I'd now become a Center City convert, it was time to explore options for another location. Almost on cue, I noticed a small sign in the front window of an upscale hair salon directly across the street at 17th and Locust. Without missing a beat, I searched out the owner and found he was looking for an upscale co-tenant who was willing to occupy the front of his salon.

The location included a storefront window and about two hundred square feet that could serve as a design studio. He was offering it at five hundred and fifty dollars a month, and at just one hundred and fifty dollars more than I had been paying for a more secluded location, I could now have a presence on one of Philadelphia's most prestigious streets. We shook hands and the deal was set.

I now had a visible location and could boast that The King's Collar Shirtmakers had widened its footprint to include a Center City, Philadelphia location. It was 1982, and it had taken me four years to come from a breakdown opening in Haddonfield New Jersey to a company that was now operating in two states.

As I look back on some of the spaces I've occupied, I'm aware that every one of them came from my focused belief that a perfect place would appear; and even to this day, there is no reason to doubt this proven phenomenon.

*Photo Credit: Stephen Tyson, 1983*

\*\*\*

I was now financially secure—and thankfully so. My daughter's father had massive health issues and soon passed away. Lisa was only eleven years' old when her dad died, and this loss was scary on many levels. While our marriage was challenging and the subsequent divorce was emotionally painful, I was now aware of the critical difference between having an ex-husband— and having a *dead* one—the term *single parent* suddenly took on an entirely new meaning.

The journey to self-sufficiency had not been easily attained, but it provided the opportunity to drive a financial future that would keep my children protected. It was also my intention to become a role model for them, and given my children's life path today and the independence they have achieved, I'm suggesting this job got done.

\*\*\*

<u>Chapter Recap</u>: Growth opportunities are often right in front of you, and when you live in *possibility*, there is always a new path to take.

# Making a Difference

By 1982, I was fully installed in my shared space in Philadelphia and able to work between the two locations, by spending three days a week at the Haddonfield Shop and three days at the Center City location.

My landlord, Guy Russell, was a member of CCAP—the Center City Association of Proprietors (its name at the time)—and encouraged me to join this small but prestigious business group. It didn't take much to enroll me. **As an activist, I am always pulled to issues that can have a positive impact on the community in which I work and live.**

I was immediately drawn to this great organization; before 1982 ended, I was elected President of The CCAP Board, a position I proudly held for sixteen years. Growing its membership became very important to me, because a large and well-respected organization has the ability to create change and growth for its business community.

Perhaps one of my special early memories was the Board Meeting called to "re-name" the group. For anyone struggling with a company name change, **a subtle change is often the best,** yet it took *many* meetings to change the name from Center City Association of Proprietors (which was always referred to as "CAP") to Center City Proprietors Association—now known as CCPA.

Even today some of its most ardent supporters remember the CAP acronym with pride. It still makes me smile that so much time was spent to remove the word "of" and shift the words around.

In a labor of love, I worked to enroll many new members, one of whom is Eugene D. McGurk, a partner at The Raynes McCarty Law Firm in Philadelphia, and Chair, Board of Advisers, Delaware Law School, Widener University. This connection provided CCPA with its meeting place, as for many years the firm hosted its monthly Board Meetings. Today, so many years later, Gene continues to serve on the CCPA Advisory Board and is a member of the Board Nominating Committee.

Gene was one of my first clients at the shared space on Locust Street, and this chance meeting led both to his involvement at CCPA, as well as his significant presence in my life. Sometimes a business connection turns into something more lasting and this chance meeting has led to a friendship that started in 1982.

Given the passion and pride I hold for both entities, I love the coincidence that The King's Collar Shirtmakers and CCAP (now CCPA), were both formed in 1978. Except for my own company, no other group captured my attention and energy as did my involvement with Center City Proprietors Association.

Through my recall of "tribal knowledge" (a phrase that refers to knowing the history of an entity) I'm happy to share some memories about this extraordinary group and acknowledge the people who first recognized the power and creativity of the entrepreneurial spirit, and the vitality it could bring to the city. (This power list of committed citizens may hold no value for those outside of the Philadelphia area, but their contributions helped to drive Philadelphia's growth.) A 2016 *Forbes* survey reported by the *The Philadelphia Business Journal* in June 2016 named Philadelphia as "the best city for millennials," and *The New York Times* revealed that Philadelphia was No. 3 in its *Top 52 Places to Go* in 2015.

Center City Philadelphia would not look the same today without the passion and vision this small group of city leaders harnessed in the 1978 working group. When it emerged, the group was dubbed *The Commissary Six* to reflect the name of organizer Steve Poses, a Center City icon who owned Frog Restaurant and The Commissary (now Frog Commissary.) He singlehandedly lit the fire that placed Philadelphia's restaurant community in the forefront of its growth. This small group of city activists also included Helen London (owner of Le Cook Nook, now of Previn Incorporated), Tom Harris (of Albert M. Greenfield Realty, now of Thomas R. Harris Real Estate), Betsy Cohen (founder of Jefferson Bank, now CEO of The Bancorp Bank), attorney Roy Yaffe (then partner at Yaffe & Golden and now partner at Gould Yaffe & Golden), and Meryl Levitz (then with Educational Resources for Business.)

As one of CCPA's original founding members, Meryl served as its Executive Director when I first became a member of the group, and chaired Board meetings that engaged our entrepreneurial spirit and gave us purpose as we worked to move Center City forward. It was an exciting time to be growing a business in the city and it was impossible to ignore her amazing organizational talents.

These talents were quickly recognized, and Meryl, who now serves as CEO and President of *Visit Philadelphia,* (previously identified as *GPTMC)* was soon off to join The Philadelphia Convention and Visitors Bureau.

A new Executive Director search soon began. Alphonse Pignataro, President of the CCPA Board and the owner of Morgan's Restaurant at the time, offered his name for that position and I was elected to fill his seat. Alphonse was the driving force in the creation of *The Restaurant Gala*, an annual event that brought the finest restaurants together to promote their best dishes, and ultimately led to the creation of the acclaimed *The Book and The Cook*. Under the direction of Judy Faye, this concept was housed at the CCPA offices, and paired nationally recognized chefs and cookbook authors for a food event that recurred for many years. I'm clear that the extraordinary Center City restaurant footprint, as we know it today, would not have evolved without CCPA and its mission to increase the vitality of Center City, Philadelphia by placing a spotlight on food as an industry.

By 1985, we held a "Trash Forum," to address the cleanliness issues in the city. At the time, Philadelphia was often referred to as *Filthydelphia,* and this first attempt at dealing with it pro-actively led to the creation of the Business District Authority and its enabling legislation that created The Center City District (CCD).

In 1986, we led the effort for a late shopping night every Wednesday, a model that would later roll out as the CCD's *Make it a Night* marketing promotion for Center City.

In 1987, working with Malcolm Lazin, a Philadelphia attorney, activist and developer, CCPA held a Bridge Lighting event at my apartment where we raised funds for the lighting of The Ben Franklin Bridge which altered the City's skyline. Once again, business came out to support its community projects.

1987 also spotlighted the *We The People 200 Governors' Ball* which represented the 200th Anniversary of the U.S. Constitution. Steve Poses, one of the original founders of CCPA and the Chef/Owner of Frog Restaurant, catered this extraordinary event. It was Steve's restaurant Frog that almost single-handedly ignited Center City's passion for eclectic dining. His contribution to this event was a testament to both his culinary skills and the vision he held for Philadelphia's emergence as the restaurant mecca it has now become. I remember standing under a tree as I witnessed the fireworks and the Governors in attendance, and became emotional at its successful conclusion. Thanks to CCPA, The Governors' Ball was the event's biggest success.

***

In 1988, our group started actively championing the creation of The Center City District, and in 1989 hired a small crew to clean the sidewalks within the CCPA boundaries. The first cleaning cart was stored at my shop, which was then located at 260 South 16th St; just next door to

Wesley Emmons, a storied jewelry designer and one of the first CAP members.

Michael Dean, an attorney at the law firm of Wolf Block LLC and now Counsel to the firm, soon asked me to join Fred Shabel, Vice Chairman of Comcast Spectacor, in the formation of the CCD working committee. I was later honored to be a Founding Officer of this remarkable and nationally recognized group when it began in 1991. Today, under the brilliant leadership of Paul Levy, the CCD has been acclaimed as a national and international model for downtown business districts.

One might think that the time spent in outside projects is time taken away from other business needs; while this is true, there's also a flip side. As President of any organization, one is held accountable by its members to listen to their issues and create solutions. It is a time-consuming position, but the paybacks are enormous. **Leading others, solving issues, and constantly working outside your comfort zone widens your network and defines your own personal growth.**

At the time, the biggest issue affecting downtown businesses was the presence of the homeless who lived on the street, sometimes even blocking a business entrance. In support of my belief that **one must always reach out to the person most equipped to handle a problem of importance**, I was pressed to reach out to Mayor W. Wilson Goode to lodge a complaint on behalf of the hundreds of businesses I was charged to represent.

Wilson Goode was Mayor during a time of great unrest in Philadelphia. Some may remember him only for the decisions made during the MOVE incident, a "lose-lose" disaster that happened during his time in office. From my view, he was simply a good man caught up in an impossible situation.

I remember walking into his office at City Hall and thinking, "I'm just a shirtmaker, what am I doing here?" As President of CCPA, I was often meeting with people I had only read about, and **there's no better finishing school than the experiences one encounters when working as a volunteer.**

**It's interesting to note that my first meeting with the Mayor started as a complaint, and ended with a solution.** (For more about Mayor Goode, go to Chapter Fourteen.)

Mayor Goode's response to our business issue was to set me up in a meeting with Sister Mary Scullion, Philadelphia's leading advocate for the marginalized community. Being with Sister Mary is a mind-blowing experience, and this meeting changed my life; she's a role model for anyone who doesn't understand the strength of **creating a solution one step at a time.**

**Many of us want change to happen NOW, and that's not the way it occurs.** It often starts with a conversation and ends with a completed project; but along the way, there are baby steps that shape the journey. Mary took me under her wing and before I knew it, I was enrolled in proactive behavior that led to a solution; in contrast to a CCPA representative with a complaint who dumped the problem in someone else's lap.

***

The homeless problem on the street was exacerbated by those in the community who gave money to the outstretched hands of those asking for food. While food was often the desired need, this money was mostly used for booze and the more money that circulated on the street, the less chance there was in getting people into shelter and on a healing path. What to do?

At the time, there were two issues that were causing grief for the city; one was the vendor cart presence on so many street corners, and the other centered on those begging for food. It was an outrageous idea, but I decided to collapse the two most hostile issues at the time and create a project that could actually solve a problem.

In 1990, when the City was looking for humane ways to treat the problem of panhandling, I formed the *I Do Care Foundation*, and authored *The Vendor Food Coupon Program* which provided vendor meals for those begging for food on the streets of Philadelphia. The food coupons could be redeemed at all Center City food vendor carts, and allowed those with humane tendencies to purchase a coupon and therefore provide an actual meal to those in need—instead of a cash handout. The food coupons were sold at every food vendor cart and twenty-seven thousand coupons were sold during its launch.

This program ultimately led to several pro-active solutions to panhandling, and eventually became a prototype for the CCD program *Make Real Change* where donated money assisted the marginalized community in real ways.

***

In a marketing blitz, CCPA continued to take the steps that would identify and promote Center City as a *Destination*. I was soon charged with doing the radio voiceovers for "There's No Shopping Center like Shopping Center City", a slogan created by Gary Levitt, a partner at the Sonder Levitt Advertising agency. This was a mantra that was repeated thousands of times over the years. Our efforts at CCPA supported a continued marketing campaign that included "More to do, More to see, More than ever: Center City Philadelphia", followed by "Center City Celebrates Style", a yearly fashion event that honored our local fashion talents.

This was a time of great growth for CCPA. It was especially rewarding for those of us who helped to move the city forward. My working partnership with Alphonse Pignataro, our Executive Director, represented teamwork at its best. Yes, CCPA had consumed me, but it had also completed me and it was time to move on.

**The test of a good business model is that it can survive without you.** The key to this is making sure you leave behind a support team with the credentials and substance to make the transition meaningful. By 1998, I had met with board member Krista Bard to explore her interest in a bigger leadership role at CCPA. The idea intrigued her and she was, in fact, a perfect match.

Krista possesses brilliant team-building skills. President of a now international business consulting company, she is a multi-accomplished, bright, and creative talent who became CCPA's driving force. Krista led CCPA for ten years. Under her able direction, she introduced her own brand of executive leadership. She was responsible for building a collaborative network of associations throughout the city, developing a sponsorship system, and nurturing the seeds of ideas I had started, shaping them into ongoing forums and event series that continued to support a healthy business climate in Center City. Among those I especially like is the *Lunch with the City's Leaders* program that she conceived to bring together leaders in every field "to provide access and insight into the powers that shape our city." This hot ticket program continues to this day.

Since 2008, the CCPA Board President has been Linda Karp, President of Karp Marketing, an award- winning certified woman-owned business, in operation since 1983. A provider of creative solutions for business marketing and development, Linda's skills continue to support CCPA programs and its advocacy for Philadelphia's small businesses. Linda is also a Professor of Graphic Design at The Art Institute of Philadelphia since 1985.

Ben Frank, CCPA's Executive Director for many years, is to be commended for his humility and gentle leadership of this great group. I close with kudos to its leaders; Past, Present, and Future, who have worked so hard to honor the vision of those who formed this association—the legacy you created *continues.*

**I have often shared the slogan that *small businesses are the engines of our economy* and when local growth is encouraged and supported, global growth can follow more easily. By their very nature, business owners possess the guts and passion needed to effect change.**

When placed in a position to make a difference, the experience often becomes an operating behavior that can serve you in many areas of your life. **The best gift of being your own "boss" is that you can shape the direction of your interests and widen your social network on your**

**own terms;** I can't imagine a better way to do this than to operate within an entrepreneurial framework and be the chooser of your life experiences.

\*\*\*

> **Chapter Recap:** Growing your business is often a by-product of the support you receive from the community-building efforts that engage and excite you. Making a difference in your community may not always increase your bottom line, but it provides the working principles and contacts that do.

CHAPTER

# 14

## Bigger is Better

While CCPA was consuming me, it also opened my eyes to the potential of an even larger business presence in Center City. Now that I had no staffing issues, I wanted to grow my company as part of that energy. The first Philadelphia studio at the Warwick Hotel was just a tease at four hundred dollars a month, but moving to the small location at 1702 Locust seemed easily doable for a more visible space, and it was only one hundred and fifty dollars more a month.

And that's when the "it's only $$$ more—why not?" phase began for me. My shared space at 1702 Locust was now in question, as my landlord wanted to sell his building. Rather than wait for this shift to occur, I decided to get pro-active and look for other possible locations in Center City. **I'm a destination-driven business, which means it's my service that drives my business, not my location.** With this thought in mind, I noticed a small space in the lobby area at The Academy House at 1420 Locust. It was easy to find, and everyone gaining access to their condo would pass by its location. I called the contact and found the rent to be just six hundred and fifty dollars a month. "Hmm"—I thought, "That's only one hundred dollars more a month."—and 1420 Locust Street soon became the third location for The King's Collar's Philadelphia presence.

It was a beautiful little shop that quickly became a destination for some of the City's most notable people; I was making shirts for Philadelphia Orchestra members and politico's that included Lieutenant Governor Bill Scranton, soon poised to run for Governor of Pennsylvania. It was a heady time for me but while beautifully appointed, it was confining and I missed the activity of a storefront location.

Almost on cue, a newspaper I hadn't ordered landed with my morning mail and I felt compelled to seek out the *space for rent* section. To my surprise (although in retrospect, that's how it always happens with me), an ad caught my attention.

An investor was looking to re-hab a brownstone into a toney apartment building requiring a storefront with panache, and he was open to do all the fit-out at his expense. The ad intrigued me—and why wouldn't it? It was an *angel gift* that got dropped in my lap and the timing was, once again, perfect. It appeared that the shop space in Haddonfield was now under attack and I needed some viable options. I had a five-year lease and a five-year option, and had just renewed my agreement, when the shopping center itself was sold. The new owners recognized they had leases that were undervalued for the price they had just paid for the property. They wanted all of us *out*. They made our lives very difficult by cutting back on maintenance, and even went so far as to not replace the lighting or do any cleaning or snow clearing.

The King's Collar was at the end of the shopping center complex and with every rain we got water in our crawl space. When the Cooper River overflowed, the spillage ended up in my shop and although we had a sump pump in the crawl space that my landlords were supposed to maintain, they stopped doing it. With no partnership from my landlords, managing the space was becoming impossible and as the threat of mold was constant, I was starting to panic.

The studio in Center City was a satellite location that was opened to increase the Company's visibility, but the Haddonfield shop housed all the inventory and the machines needed to make our product. This was the space I had to protect.

**I've always been a "safety net" person and will often create that landing space in advance of any perceived need. Any new opportunity can be an exit strategy if one becomes necessary, and I was intrigued.**

The owner of the building was a quirky friendly man and our meeting went exceptionally well. He was looking to re-fit the space to my specifications and willing to spend some serious money to do so. The rental package also included the two bedroom first floor apartment which could be sublet, thus making my lease amount very manageable. The total package was seventeen hundred and fifty dollars a month, and given that I could get at least one thousand dollars rent for the apartment, my actual shop rent would be just one hundred dollars more than my present location. I thought, "Only one hundred dollars more? Why not?"

It's interesting to note that while I still had a lease at 1420 Locust Street, **I also knew I had the option to find a new tenant to replace me, should I decide to end my lease without penalty; a caveat I always wrote into my leases.** This was an option I was about to use and it served me well—I was able to find another tenant and leave with integrity.

I was now about to move again, and this time, into a brand new space that was just next door to Wesley Emmons Jeweler's, a CCPA member having a strong following as a jewelry designer for some of the area's most successful families. My new landlord was excited about our artistic match for his building and the deal was set. My new address would now be 260 South 16th Street in Center City, Philadelphia and it was time to share the news with the Haddonfield staff.

I called my New Jersey landlords with the news that should they want to re-capture my space, I'd be willing to vacate. I offered to not stay out my lease if they would just give me enough money to cover my moving costs. I had expected a positive response, but their answer was shocking.

"Nancy, we have no intention to pay anyone to move. We will allow you to break your lease and not charge you a termination fee, and given that you're already motivated, we need an answer *ASAP.*" They knew I couldn't remain with the maintenance issues they were causing and they were forcing my hand.

Thankfully, I already had a new possibility and a brand new beautiful building was being re-fit to my specifications. **My safety net was already in place.**

**For me, "Deciding to decide" holds the space for miracles.**

My sister Joan often reminds me that "good luck" is often just a reflection of "paying attention and showing up." This life view was shared by her religious coach and it has become the light bulb that continues to brighten my journey, as I wander down the entrepreneurial path.

This larger space signified the company's transition from a start-up to a stable company. Its Center City location was the perfect match for a shop serving an upscale clientele, and became identified as an "atelier" selling a bespoke product that would soon have the following I had always anticipated.

*Photo credit: The Philadelphia Inquirer 1986*

\*\*\*

It's interesting to note that I started my company during a time when the economy was at its harshest. The early 1980's were financially challenging, but I seemed to have had blinders on; I viewed my business only through the eyes of those who could afford my product. **It never occurred to me that I would fail;** I'd already survived the loss of my original partner at start-up and I had become fearless.

Even in a challenging economy, some people always have money, and **entrepreneurs often weigh many decisions out of the passion they hold for their vision.** It was during this time that I was approached and asked to consider a *Made to Measure* shirt service; I liked the idea, but I must admit I was still a snob at the time and I declined.

I was making a *bespoke* product, meaning the fabrics were in-house, and each person had a hand drawn paper pattern that was used to cut the cloth by hand, each shirt sewn one at a time. I held a sense of pride about all these steps and felt I was creating meaningful work for my staff members. I was a local company making an American-made product and I would not ever consider an off-shore manufacturing source.

By the late 1980's, the economy started warming up again and signaled the rise of discretionary spending. While *Bespoke* custom shirts were once only a concept to be considered by those with deeper pockets, this special service now included a *Made to Measure* product and opened the door for a larger audience. It appeared a perfect time to consider this new option.

The Company that originally approached me was Individualized Shirts, a division of The Individualized Apparel Group, and in (another) twist of fate, its CEO Joe Blair was a former Custom Shop employee—a powerful bond. We met at my studio and I showed him the steps we took to make our bespoke product. I remember saying, "I employ people here and that's important to me. I want American–made to make a difference." And I remember his response. "Nancy, we're a manufacturer of a product made in our New Jersey workrooms. I want you to spend some time there and that may help you with your decision." This was a big shift for me, both emotionally and financially, and the conflict was enormous.

I agreed to spend a day at the factory. It was a day that altered my professional life, as the experience proved to be a mind-changer. Everything I did in my small space with a handful of people was replicated by their state of the art machines. I witnessed perhaps one hundred and sixty staff members working at their cutting and sewing stations. As I watched the process, I was blown away by the pride they all held in the services they performed. I went from cutting stations to sewing stations, to the finishing of the product; it was indeed a custom product that was still American-made. By using this company and adding this service to my own, I could still make a difference.

The country had just come through a recession and spending was heating up again. I soon recognized that I was now serving two different groups of people: those who had big incomes and those who had HUGE incomes. **Watching a trend develop is an important step in any entrepreneurial venture,** and having spent almost fifteen years growing an upscale business, I recognized that alternative shopping options might be something worth pursuing. Suddenly shops like Walmart and Kmart and a plethora of stores that sold housewares, building supplies and discount clothing for men and women were emerging—a trend worth considering.

This day at the factory changed the direction of the company by recognizing the move toward careful spending. It also allowed us to provide services that included both *Bespoke* and *Made to Measure* custom shirts, yet still honored the pride The King's Collar has always held as a company with USA roots. In a big shout-out to this remarkable company, the stand they've taken to keeping it real and to steadfastly offer an American-made product has made a lasting difference across our country to other shop owners. As of 2016, this wonderful American company carries a factory staff of two hundred and forty people. The King's Collar has evolved as one of their longest standing accounts, and the service they provide to emerging businesses that include a shirtmaking component has been enormous.

**Offering a new path, and telling someone about its importance does not have the same power as showing someone how it's achieved.**

The decision to offer a full-service option for custom shirts by including this new direction was a break-through moment for the company. I could now add a service that included very little start-up costs and a product line that supported the concept that **all businesses should use every square foot of their space to generate income.** There was a steady stream of business, and clients enjoyed the upscale ambiance and the little pocket of privacy that provided a comfortable and unhurried sales experience.

\*\*\*

One of these clients was Mayor W. Wilson Goode (see also, Chapter 18) and the first fitting was both rewarding and humorous. He arrived in a private car. With a bodyguard stationed at the front door, he proceeded into the back fitting area where I was able to do the required measurements. As I was finishing up the taping, I flipped up his collar to get his neck size and noticed that inside his collar stay pockets were two bobby pins. This just made me giggle, and I remember saying, "Nice touch!" I have often wondered if that was an appropriate comment to make to any client, let alone the Mayor of your city, but it landed well, and he just smiled at me. (I actually thought it was a pretty clever idea.)

I had always liked this Mayor and although he served during one of Philadelphia's most challenging times, for me, it was not the MOVE altercation that defined him, it was his inherent goodness that was a match for his name. It was he who introduced me to Sister Mary Scullion at *Project Home,* and he set up meetings where we could assist those in the marginalized community find a better life. When I was honored to receive the Inc. Magazine Entrepreneur of the Year Award as a "socially responsible business owner," he attended and sat with our family.

\*\*\*

The shop on 16th Street was indeed magical. My days were spent selling shirts for *Made to Measure* and *Bespoke* orders, and my nights were spent drawing patterns and prepping work for our cutter. I was finally comfortable in a space, I had a staff I respected, and I was living my dream when my landlord reminded me that it was time to negotiate the lease renewal. By this time, I had moved into the apartment that was part of the leased space.

While the apartment itself was beautifully done, it was always dark and I started suffering from light deprivation. The only thing that made the lease work was the perk of the attached apartment, and I no longer wanted to live there. I didn't want the stress of taking on a sub-lease tenant, and it appeared I was now facing the possibility of another move. This is never an easy decision, but sometimes life pushes you in a direction that you might otherwise not take, and I was again faced with exploring an option I had not anticipated.

***

---

**Chapter Recap**: Growing your business includes making decisions that often fall outside your comfort zone. Whether it's taking a chance on a larger space, or creating a different concept for your business, growth always comes from a new possibility.

---

# CHAPTER 15

## The Staff of (Work) Life

The 16th Street location had panache. The staff loved the space in the trendy location and the work stations provided a comfortable place where we became our creative best.

As the years passed, The King's Collar attracted a dedicated work staff that took great pride in the special service we provided. Some used the time to hone their skills and create their own future, and just as I had been given the chance to define my own, I was happy to pay it forward.

I had asked the Haddonfield staff to relocate to the Philadelphia shop and Michel Karkar, who had started with us in Haddonfield, was happy to do so. His contribution to our company was rooted in the timing of his hire; a new cutter I had hired to replace the one who had been so insubordinate did not have the required skills, and I had already decided to let him go. Just then Michel's uncle stopped by the Haddonfield shop to see if I was open to hiring an experienced shirtmaker. **Timing is everything.**

Several of his family members had been killed in the bombing of Beirut and as a non-political visa holder he needed a safe place to land. I was pulled to help if I could. His inquiry came at a perfect time and I told him I'd be open to an interview. Michel soon came by and I was mesmerized by this young man who held himself with so much pride. He had been trained as a shirtmaker in Beirut, loved his craft, and had the presence of someone many years older. It was my intention to sponsor him when we moved to Center City so he could remain here, but the paper work was hard to do; when an opportunity came up that eventually took him to Toronto, he left our company to start his new life. I mention him by name because he has since built a company of his own and has become one of Toronto's most sought after custom designers. He came to us at a time when we both needed each other, and to this day, we continue our friendship.

One of my most dedicated operators, Adele Stachiotti, was unable to make the move. I hated having to replace her, but it was necessary. When Brenda Dempster responded to my ad, I was immediately drawn to her talent and her life story. She was raising her children alone; I could identify. Brenda adapted beautifully to her new operator position, but some weeks after hiring her, she told me she was pregnant. She knew this when I offered her the job but she chose not to share this information, fearing I'd deny her the opportunity.

My first thought was "Now what? Will I spend the next few months training her, only to replace her after the birth of her child? And if she returned, how could we survive so many weeks without staff support?"

It was that thought that had me look at my *present* moment, as I recognized that what happens in that space is all that's really important.

**So many times, one worries about future upsets and losses, while failing to value the gift in front of them.** Brenda needed this job to support her family, and as I recognized this behavior from my own personal history, I knew I'd keep her on staff and trust G-d to provide the next step.

The months passed and as Brenda's belly got bigger, so did my trepidation about the choice I had made. Brenda assured me that she would work until just before her delivery and without missing a beat, I said "I will keep your job open, if you promise you will return as quickly as possible." And we agreed to honor our commitment to one another.

Brenda left to have her baby and the orders began to pile up. As I was starting to feel pressure about our delivery delay, I called all the clients affected and alerted them about this probability until we were able to get back on a better schedule. **A critical part of keeping a company viable is communicating with your client base when outside issues arise.** Once again, everyone understood, but I had no idea how I would handle this staffing problem. I was starting to panic when *another* "gift from the universe" suddenly appeared.

I received a call from Eugene Caringel, a voice from the past, who wanted to know if I was hiring. **Yes, timing is everything,** and in one of my darkest hours, I was hearing from someone who could easily step in and get us back on schedule.

In a quirky reminder that **Karma is often life's best teacher,** I tell you that Eugene was the man who had called me ten years before looking for an operator position when I was in Haddonfield. At that time, I had just filled the position he was applying for (I had just hired Del) but I had given him a contact and a reference for a company in New York. He now shared that my letter of recommendation had allowed him to work at that company for all those years. (I had forgotten I had even done that.)

He told me that the New York commute had become a hardship for him and he felt compelled to reach out to me once again. I hired Gene immediately and had the honor and pleasure to work with him until he was in his 80's. He was a gifted operator and sometimes his work was so beautifully sewn that it made me cry. When one is in the presence of this kind of talent, one is indeed blessed.

Gene worked at 16th Street until just days before he died peacefully in his sleep. A life well lived.

Brenda returned to the company after the birth of her child and became the longest working staff member in the company. Some eighteen years later, Brenda succumbed to cancer and the loss was hard to accept. Those who own businesses may recognize that relationships formed during the work day are often more intimate than those shared with friends, and even some family members. In a tightly held company, a work "family" shares many hours together. Losses are deeply felt, **and the synergy created by a cohesive staff is the glue that holds a company together.**

As entrepreneurs, we have the opportunity to live life by our own rules. Many of these rules come from lessons learned and losses endured, but the most rewarding is having experienced the power of mentoring and then remembering to pay it forward.

Just as I was given a life-changing opportunity when I was first hired by Alan Bresnick at The Custom Shop, I had found myself in a position to pay it forward with the hiring of Michel Karkar and now that I needed a critical staff member to cover for Brenda, the reference I had offered to Gene Caringel so many years earlier, brought him back at a time when I needed him most.

***

**Chapter Recap:** Whenever one is placed in a position to serve as a mentor, it should be welcomed. Every mentoring opportunity I shared came back positively—often in unexpected ways. Mentoring has become a key component of our company's growth and longevity. Creating the perfect staff is sometimes harder (and sometimes easier) then one might expect.

# CHAPTER 16

# Coming Full Circle

In looking for another location for The King's Collar, I continued to trust a higher power to lead me and I remained confident that the perfect space would appear.

I was used to paying a higher rent due to the added apartment at the 16th Street location, but because I had just secured a new living space for less money, I had some wiggle room. On an afternoon walk, I noticed a new FOR RENT sign at 1704 Walnut Street and it caught me by surprise. It had not been there the day before and I was now looking at a location that held great significance.

As the reader, you may be picking up a strong spiritual connection, and it's this strong faith that continues to define and support me. Coincidences have shaped my life in powerful ways and I sometimes think the choices we make are based on a pre-set destiny. As you continue to read this chapter, you will note the "coincidence" that blew me away.

In 1965, I had walked through the front door of The Custom Shop Shirtmakers at 1700 Walnut Street to apply for a salesgirl position; by the early 1990's, I was President of King's Collar Shirtmakers and considering a space that was just two doors away from my first job. The expression "meant to be" flashed before me, and I knew that 1704 Walnut would be my next location.

This street-front address included two huge display windows on Walnut Street and I was excited by the possibility of showing the wonderful merchandise we so proudly offered. I found I had an innate talent for window displays that pulled people into our shop, cultivated during my seven years at The Custom Shop that involved breaking down a display and creating the interest for new merchandise. Many of the tasks I had observed and helped shape during those early years as a sales person, came back as a *how-to* moment I was able to replicate for my own company. **I'm thinking it's wise to pay attention to EVERYTHING in your work life, as the job you hold as an employee can shape the enterprise you may one day create under your own identity.**

I had hoped that our street-front location at 1704 Walnut Street would be our final destination, but **business changes often occur that make you re-think your operation,** and the fashion industry was headed in a new direction.

The 1990s included a wave of prosperity and this address was a perfect match for the interest held in our product. We happily rode that wave until changes in the custom shirt industry began affecting the need for this service.

It was a hard landing.

*Dress Down Friday* had morphed into Casual Dress on many more days of the week. The dress shirt business took a huge hit. As I witnessed this phenomenon, I realized that it actually came out of the greed that some in our industry held about increasing market share. **When you come from greed, your true purpose is often placed in jeopardy.**

Since dress shirts were always strong, some leaders in the industry felt that adding a casual component would *increase* profits. They had envisioned a look that included button down shirts, patch elbow blazers, slacks and loafers, and felt this would be an added product that would increase sales. What showed up were jeans and sneakers and golf shirts. The beautifully well-dressed man wearing custom suits and shirts, silk ties and pocket squares was soon replaced by the dot.com dress-down in which consultants felt more comfortable.

The street-front space at 1704 was beautiful and the toney address was certainly a draw, but **when you see a trend, it's always wise to pay attention. (One may notice by now that *trend-following* is a theme that runs through-out this narrative, and it's important to note its inclusion—and importance.)**

I now had to re-think my finances and come up with a solution that would allow us to cover all the expenses of a product that was locally made. My costs have always been significant because I take great pride in manufacturing a product that is USA made, and I have never sold anything that wasn't made in America. This position is so strong for me that I've always created a budget around fulfilling this mission.

The building itself was wonderful, and I had quickly connected with the other tenants who shared space on the upper floors. One of these tenants was Lee Wybranski, an artist whose niche was golf, and as two of my sons are PGA Golf Pros, this connection was delicious for me. At the time, he was just starting out and I would end my days by meeting him upstairs to watch him at his drawing table. He would make paintings of notable holes on some of the nation's most acclaimed golf courses, and his talent was so spot-on that I just knew he'd be a super star someday. His technique was truly amazing and so carefully drawn that I would tell him I could almost see the grass growing.

As entrepreneurs, we shared many of our stories and I noted this connection is often a big part of growing your own business; only another entrepreneur can understand the highs and lows of what's at risk when you take a leap of faith. (As of 2016, Lee has evolved into the one of the premier golf artists in the country; his collectible work reflects commissions from *The*

*PGA of America* and *The United States Golf Association.* He has done, and continues to create, the posters for every major golf tournament including *The U.S. Open.*)

After I closed my shop, I would buzz his bell and go down the long hallway to the building elevator that would take me to his upstairs studio. The entrance door to the business located in the rear of the building was next to the elevator and advertised as a Salon, but I soon noted it was actually a massage parlor that offered "special" services—on Walnut Street no less! This was unacceptable and as I was very connected in city politics at that time, I made a call to License and Inspections, and in a short while the door was barricaded and the business was closed.

And that's when an important *ah ha!* moment happened. Why not move to the back space? The rent was *half* of what I had been paying, yet nothing else needed to change. I could keep my phone, stationary, checkbook and all the print material that reflected my present business at 1704 Walnut Street.

I called my landlord, Stanley Solo, to explore this possibility and as a Walnut Street address was starting to once again hold the panache it deserved, we both knew that finding a tenant for the storefront space would be easy to do. I asked him to meet me at the building so I could walk through the back space and see if it could serve our needs. As we were walking down the long hallway, my landlord said to me, "It's so interesting you want this space for your business as it was the first location for The John Shaw Company."

Say what?

He shared this was the actual space that served as the business address for my father's shirtmaker so many years before—**indeed, this was the same hallway I walked down to pick up my Dad's custom shirts when I was just twelve years' old**—*coincidence?*

It seemed to me my career must have started at age ten when I proudly noticed the monogram on my dad's custom shirt, followed by my being asked to pick up his order at this same Walnut Street studio at age twelve. Thirteen years later, I had answered an ad in a newspaper I hadn't ordered, was hired as a salesgirl at The Custom Shop to sell haberdashery, was soon trained as a shirt designer because someone recognized that women needed to be included in the industry, and was then moved into management because a key employee was called to the Priesthood. In 1978, just six years after I was fired from this job that helped define my career, I opened my own shirt company in Haddonfield; and by the late 1990s, I was occupying the same space as my father's shirtmaker from so many years before, just two doors down from my first job.

This was a journey that took almost fifty years to complete; as I walked through the space, I was reminded that my career choice must have been inevitable, based on the coincidences that preceded it. I think the "coincidences" in my life are so prevalent because I trust the Universe to provide and in my worst moments, there's always a gift. Some of the harshest incidents in my life have opened up a path to the best imaginable experiences.

I did make the shift from street-front to the large working studio at ground floor rear. The move was internal, I lost no business, I was able to sublet the street-front space until my actual lease ended, and everyone's needs were met.

This is a story I could never have made up. Truth is indeed stranger than fiction. It's now clear I have traveled a path that appeared to be pre-set for me, and this has caused me to wonder if our lives are indeed drawn for us long before we live them.

Some may think these thoughts are nonsense, but not in my world. I believe that resistance can shut the door to the magic that's possible, and that when you stay open to the gifts your thoughts generate, it's possible to live in a space of miracles. It's been said one should be careful what one wishes for, as your wish might come true. I have always tried to envision scenarios that have no malice toward others and provide the opportunity to live into beliefs that only support a higher good. It has worked for me, and I posit it may work for you.

**Try to keep your thoughts pure, and *always* come from integrity.**

\*\*\*

**Chapter Recap**: Thoughts *indeed* are THINGS. Look around your life and you may be able to recognize that what fills that life is a reflection of your deepest and sometime silent hopes and dreams.

# The Millennium Shift

Perhaps it's an entrepreneurial drive to just keep moving.

When I was fired in 1972 because of my gender, it hadn't occurred to me that I'd have my own company just six years later. Growing the business certainly had its bad days and great days, but the approaching Millennium had me re-think my options. At age sixty, I was now looking for a different business model, and I made the decision to re-create my life when I noticed that our Center City business had become a four-day business only.

Many years before, I decided to close on Mondays. Working five days a week was my limit and Saturday was always a strong sales day. This was the case when we had the shop in Haddonfield, but while our Center City clientele worked in the City, many had homes on The Main Line, Chester County, or in affluent New Jersey communities; Saturday business was no longer as strong.

With the millennium approaching, I felt that if I always did what I always did, I'd always get what I always got, and as the year 2000 began, I wanted to do something *dramatic*—and I did. Within a six-week window, I sold and moved from my Center City condo, closed the Walnut Street location, and established King's Collar Shirtmakers in Ardmore—Whew.

**It was Ardmore's location that called out to me.** As I was driving down
Lancaster Avenue to the country one weekend, I drove through the town
and noted that several of my Walnut Street neighbors had satellite stores on
Ardmore's signature shopping block. I passed Pearl of the East, Robinson
Luggage, Robbins Jewelers and Jacques Ferber Furs, all businesses I had
worked with during my tenure as President of Center City Proprietors
Association. Continuing down Lancaster Avenue, I noticed Past Present
Future, a gift store filled with wonderful and whimsical crafts and toys,
owned by Sherry Tillman. Sherry was one of my CCPA colleagues whom
I met when her shop was originally located on 19th street in Center City.
Her budding business seemed to blossom in the town of Ardmore, so when
I saw a small store for rent located just next door to The Ardmore Movie
Theatre, I knew I had found my perfect location. I contacted the realtor,
and the agreement was in place.

In looking back at the timing, I'm aware that **change can be a well-
planned event, or as in my case, an intuitive response to a pivotal
time in history.** It was also made possible by a healthy and growing real
estate market in 2000 that allowed me to sell my Center City condo with
simply a note on the laundry room bulletin board, no realtor fee, and a one
hundred percent profit on a property I had purchased just two years before.

Who would have thought this real estate "gift" would one day create the
market crash that followed some years later? But you'll have to keep reading
to see how this all landed for me. The move to the suburbs was not only
a location change, but also a life style change. During my Center City
years, I didn't own a car, and the social calendar of our city business kept
me captive without one. I now felt myself pulled to a life with less stress
and more free time.

This was a feeling that had been cultivated by finding a little creek-side
cottage in the late 1990s that has become a spiritual retreat for myself
and my family. In fact, there are still marks on the wall that measured
my grandsons' height from the time they were four years old. The place
has added balance to my life and created the healing respite that had me
considering a slower pace. The move to the suburbs was actually rooted

in having found this special cottage, although I certainly wasn't aware of it at the time.

With the condo money in the bank, and a perfect new location that would support my client base, I decided to rent an apartment on the Main Line until I became comfortable with the change in my new life style. I quickly found an apartment nearby and signed the lease on my way to the cottage. I was barely past the Ardmore city line, when just three blocks down the road, I saw a *For Sale* sign on a small house that appeared to be empty. I felt myself being pulled onto the driveway and peered inside to find a perfect little home, just several blocks from the site of the storefront that held so much possibility. I wrote down the realtor's number, called the rental office and rescinded my lease offer. Without even knowing its price, I knew this home was meant to be mine.

I connected with the realtor that Sunday, and found it was an estate transaction that included bad family vibes that had delayed its sale. I was given the price and decided to offer the exact amount I had just made in my condo sale and not a penny more. The house had been abandoned, and the timing was perfect for a low-ball offer.

By now, you may recognize that my decisions are made quickly because **when something feels right, I act on it.** The next day my offer was accepted and I was now a homeowner. As 2000 started, I had a wonderful business location on the Main Line, a home that provided ease and peace in my life, and a business bottom line that was healthy and growing.

…And then our world crumbled.

On September 11th 2001, as I was walking to the shop with my son Ira, my neighbors reported that the World Trade Towers had been hit by a plane. As many do, I remember that day, the fear and loss that colored it, and the recognition that our lives would be changed forever. This unexpected event caught us all off balance. Lives were lost, fortunes disappeared, and no one could guess how it would turn out. The concept of *Fear* returned to my life, and it stayed there. Market forces crushed us. and just one year after a life-changing business move, my perfect location soon became less so. Over a short period of time, the businesses that pulled me there closed or moved. The movie theatre shut down. Sherry Tillman and I were the only original stores from our CCPA shared history that were left on a block that had showed such potential.

**It was time for out of the box thinking—again.**

The store was a block long, with a front door access and a back door that abutted one of Ardmore's largest parking lots. Even with a beautiful storefront, almost everyone who entered came in through the back entrance. Many years before, this location had actually served two businesses, so the back and the front each had separate utility boxes. It occurred to me that I could operate as just a studio by walling off the back area and subletting the front. I offered this idea to my landlord and as they could now have two tenants paying rent in the same space, they were happy to be presented with this possibility.

My company was in the process of getting smaller, yet I was still able to provide the same service. Surviving the September 11th nightmare was my only motivation. **Maybe bigger isn't always better.** I became obsessed with finding ways that could protect me from the whims and constraints of outside forces.

Real estate was *hot*. As it turned out for many, too hot, but I was one of the lucky ones because I was able to turn a real-estate frenzy into the making of a meaningful business decision. In 2005, I found Liz Fondren, a realtor who continues to be my friend, and asked her to be on the look-out for a commercial property that could serve as a fallback location should I never need it. The request led to a call to action, and within days she alerted me to a duplex that was zoned as a commercial property and located just across the parking lot from my studio's location.

As an active business owner, and at the time, President of The Ardmore Business Association, I knew Ardmore's stakeholders. The owner of the building was someone I had interacted with on community projects. **I have always been actively involved in the communities in which I do business; this connection came directly from being involved**

**and therefore knowing whom to contact** and how best to get a speedy response. **As a business owner, who you know is always your access to getting your needs met** and the time spent in community projects can often open doors that may be closed to others.

I reached him immediately and since timing was critical, I asked that he not put the sale sign up. I was ready to make an offer. **I wanted him to know I was a serious buyer, so I offered him five thousand dollars above his asking price,** told him I was already pre-approved, and could make an immediate settlement. It was an offer he couldn't refuse.

**Sometimes offering *more* than a posted price is exactly the formula needed when you want to insure a positive outcome.** Within thirty days, I was an off-site landlord for the two tenants who held leases in the building, and I had secured a commercial address should the need again surface.

The sale happened during those ridiculous days when anyone could buy real estate and could do so with very little money. I've always been a believer in "keeping it on the block", and *shopping local* gives one the chance to help another business and also establish a meaningful working relationship with someone who actually knows your name. I was also lucky to be working with a client of mine, Pat Keenan, the Branch Manager at Wells Fargo Home Mortgage and the sale was handled with speed, integrity, and accuracy. At the time, I was able to secure the exact space I needed to insure my future with just ten percent down and a quick settlement. I paid top dollar for the building, but **sometimes the cost of owning something pales in relationship to the need for owning it.**

This is a sale that ultimately shaped my present life, as it generated the thoughts and actions that followed and prepped the "safety net" that continues to support me to this day.

Retail is tough.

There are great days and there are days when one wonders how bills can get paid. The roller coaster of owning a business may hold no interest for the faint of heart, but for those brave creative souls who define challenge as an opportunity for growth, **there is nothing more rewarding than creating something out of *nothing*.** Moving from one location to another was simply the next step. **When running a company, standing still can be a killer when one pays no attention to outside forces.**

In looking back over my finances, the shift from Center City to the suburbs was barely recognizable, as the figures actually showed an increase immediately following this abrupt and unexpected move. This, once again, confirmed that I am the Kings Collar Company, wherever I am; it's not about where the business is located. **By tracking and keeping my clients informed, I have been able to move from location to location, without severe business losses, because I prep these moves with the marketing outreach that keeps us connected.**

***

> **Chapter Recap:** Every business needs an insurance policy of some kind that covers theft, fire and water, and liability damage, but the most important consideration is the *thinking* that can provide a solution for a completely unexpected incident. Owning is always better than renting when you want to secure a future you can control.

# 18

—◦◦◦◦—

# The Housing Crash

When I moved from Center City in 2000, I had already served as President of the CCPA Board for sixteen years. Upon landing in the suburbs, I found that The Ardmore Business Association was struggling to find its own voice. As a community activist, I was pulled to one of its meetings and before I knew it, I had placed my name on the ballot to serve as its President and won the election. While Ardmore was pressing for its own growth prior to 2001, this terrorist attack on the nation's economy was an even bigger assault on Ardmore's presence, and the town was filled with empty storefronts.

Ardmore's future was in question.

**One can rail against a debilitating issue, or one can be pro-active in finding solutions,** and the effort to revitalize Ardmore became a critical part in shaping the future of my own company. I wanted to organize the businesses in a way that called for a path to re-birth, and I reached out to business owner Christine Vilardo who had moved her company Aqua Hut from the town of Manayunk, at the same time I moved from Center City. We were fellow business owners who both saw the potential for Ardmore; I asked her to serve as Vice-President of the ABA Board, and work with me to help grow its membership. We then added Larry Gee, who at the time was GM of the Suburban Square Shopping Center, credited with being one of the first shopping centers in the United States. Ardmore's commercial district has always been home to the "mom and pop" stores that offer the goods and services upon which its residents rely; we felt it was important to link and unite Ardmore's downtown business district to this toney lifestyle center, in an effort to drive Ardmore as a "Destination."

As the years passed, Christine became a colleague and a friend, and by the time I stepped down from the ABA Board, Christine's leadership acumen led to her present position as Executive Director of The Ardmore Initiative, (A.I.) Ardmore's Business District Authority.

A.I. was originally named Ardmore 2000 by community leaders Charlie Ward—who had served as Board President for The Lower Merion Board of Commissioners (BOC)—and Mike Silver—an Ardmore stakeholder and the named partner of his Firm, Silver and Silver Attorneys at Law. They felt that a name change and a new Executive Director were needed. We were well past the year 2000 and we all felt a new identity would move us forward. By this time, I had also joined as a Board Director and just as I was privy to the name change at CCPA, I was also part of Ardmore's naming team. We chose The Ardmore Initiative to reflect the efforts we expected to generate, a name that has served us well.

As a back story, when we were discussing names, I remembered working with Mayor Wilson Goode to achieve a break-through in the Center City, Philadelphia's homeless population. He formed (and named) The Center City Homeless Initiative and appointed me Chair of the Committee. It was the Mayor's vision to create pro-active solutions to address panhandling and the humane housing of Center City's marginalized community.

The word *Initiative* captured the work that lay before us. I always loved that word for the *possibility* it represented, and there was agreement that it would be a match for Ardmore's new direction.

Now under Christine Vilardo's stewardship The Ardmore Initiative began to lead the community on its new path. Christine is that rare individual who can live in two worlds, both as a business owner and a community leader. She's feisty, fair, and formidable and in her leadership role as Executive Director of The Ardmore Initiative, we are blessed to have her fighting with and for us as we continue to encourage new development, and create Ardmore's revitalization.

It has been a long and difficult journey but Ardmore has since become one of the Main Line's premier destinations for empty-nester's, as well as millennials. One Ardmore Place, the long awaited and hard-fought Carl Dranoff mixed-use project at fifty-six million dollars, has been slated for completion by 2018. A transit-friendly project, it has already attracted other investors to consider Ardmore's location as one that holds great promise. As my property abuts this Cricket Lot footprint that offers such potential, I'm clear that my purchase in 2005 will ultimately prove to be a wiser decision than I had anticipated at the time.

***

I ultimately left the ABA Board. In 2008 I was honored to win The First Annual "Charlie" Award, as exemplified by Charles F. Ward for his "selflessness, integrity, leadership and kindness" for the stand he took in moving Ardmore forward. I cherish this award because my heart really does belong to Ardmore.

It was now time, however, to put my attention on my own company. By the start of 2008, we had begun to recover our business footing. The path was arduous, yet in a surprising move, each step I have taken since that horrific day in September 2001 was a step that made my life *smaller*.

**As the years passed, the only way our company was able to survive was by paying careful attention to the market forces,** and accessing belt tightening opportunities that saved us money while still generating an income. I found I had a real knack for driving our own PR, and I created an in-house media company that controlled and promoted our business message without paying an outside agency. I soon found that I was developing a small following of other business owners who asked that I assist them with their own message, and The King's Writer division was born.

**Entrepreneurs often possess the creative gifts they relegate to others, yet while outsourcing is a great possibility, sometimes the best messenger is the one who has the most at risk.**

I'm also a business owner who now provides (and takes) coaching, as **it's what we don't know that we don't know that gets us in trouble.** Many years before, in 1978, when I was first shaping The King's Collar Shirtmakers in Haddonfield New Jersey, my son Bob cautioned me to learn everything I could about the product I made. By 2008, I had taught myself how to design a shirt, draw a pattern, cut an order, hand draw a monogram, present an appealing store window display, personally manage PR and Marketing, and handle all the payroll and bookkeeping that drove my business. I was unable to sew, but I always told the staff that even if I didn't know *how* to do it, I knew *what* to do and could direct them appropriately. I hired the best of the best and I trained every staff member personally.

By 2008, our small studio was generating a comfortable income, I had a home nearby and a commercial building with two tenants who paid rents that carried the mortgage on the property. I was living comfortably when the downstairs tenant moved unexpectedly, and I was starting to feel the stress of finding another person to fill the space. And I suddenly thought—why not *me?*

I was living alone in a house I owned, the market was crazy, the prices for homes in the area was off the charts, and **I wondered if the trend would continue. What if it didn't?** This is "the little voice" that my mom always urged me to honor. She gave me a small sign written by Caroline Joy Adams that reflects this wisdom and it resides by my bedside. **"LISTEN to your inner voice… TRUST your intuition, your deep inner wisdom… for when the time is right, your heart will always tell you what you seek to know."**—The voice was saying, "Sell now."

I called my realtor Liz Fondren, did some clean-up curb appeal, and within two months sold the house at double the price I had paid just eight years before. By the end of the summer, I was living in the first floor apartment of my duplex, directly across the parking lot from my down-sized studio. The next step was to lower the mortgage on *this* building. I called the bank and re-set my mortgage to three and a half percent, and transferred the money from the house sale to pay down its balance.

I now had my finances in place and could start to again build back the business lost over the previous years. I had already made significant progress by 2007, and as 2008 began I was confident I had taken every step possible to insulate the company from any other possible loss. 2008 was now on track to being my best year since the free-fall of 2001. That "little voice" had saved me and I had now landed in a space that I could easily afford.

**The key to keeping a business viable is to rigorously watch your expenses**. There will always be fixed costs, but it's not always what you're spending that matters, it's what you're *saving* by making smarter choices. Even when buying inventory, **your bottom line increases by how smart you are about your purchasing costs,** and not always by how much you are charging your clients for the product. By carefully monitoring my expenses, I passed along the savings to my clients by not raising prices, even though my factory was compelled to do so in order to cover their own operating expenses.

Over the years, I had taken every step possible to contain my costs while continuing to market my services. In every economy there are those who make money, and my product was always appreciated by those who had discretionary funds to spend. Our company had a great reputation and our client base was loyal and supportive. As the summer ended, I felt we were back on track.

And then in September 2008—the housing market collapsed.

Had I not acted on that "little voice" my mom always cautioned me to respect, I would have missed the selling window that doubled my money. The King's Collar now had a solid business location that offered stability, a soft landing should the need ever arise, and our future was finally secure.

***

-------------------------------------------------------------

**Chapter Recap**: The business world revolves around many issues that are candidly out of its control. The best you can do is build a business model that includes a concept worth supporting, a trained and well-paid staff who are positioned to deliver a product of merit, and a critical eye towards framing and refining the cost to do business when outside influences come at you unexpectedly.

-------------------------------------------------------------

# CHAPTER 19

## The Studio Conversion

I note with interest that the first location for The King's Collar had a back entrance to a parking lot, and in this sense we were back to our beginnings many moves later. Parking access has always been critical, and **as an appointment-only business, it's the convenience that matters.** The small studio space was easily fulfilling its need, and with a living space just directly across the parking lot, I felt that our business formula was in place.

I was on a month to month lease and the space was so perfectly suited to our needs that I felt safe. With just four hundred square feet and a rear location off a parking lot, there was no foot traffic per se, so I felt confident we could easily remain there. My landlord was collecting rent from two tenants, each at more money than my original lease cost; the rear location was an ideal studio location for us, but perhaps not so ideal for someone else.

—Or so I thought.

We had made the back area so inviting, that my landlord now felt they could get more rent for it. They floated the idea that they would be increasing the rent and would be looking for a tenant who could be charged twice the amount we had been paying.

My good idea had come back to bite us.

I'm sure they felt I would have to comply—my business depended on a stable location, i.e. *this* one—but I was no longer held captive by my landlord's whim. I now had complete control over our company's future because I had created an alternative location, and with a property just across the way, we could decline the offer. As a courtesy, I gave my landlord sixty days' notice to find another tenant and began the task of prepping the commercial property to also include our new in-house workrooms.

The basement was dry, clean, and had high ceilings. John B. Gregory & Sons is a local contractor in whom I had confidence, and we designed the space that would easily house our sewing machines, cutting tables and the shelving for all the fabrics. As I write this, John and I still work together so many years later. **Over the years, I found I was creating a go-to list of providers**, and every one of them are still people I can trust to follow my instructions and work with integrity.

The space was shaping up perfectly, and the upstairs studio soon reflected the look of a comfortable European *Atelier*. It was cozy and inviting and hopefully a welcome respite for my clients who were used to a toney location, but could now also enjoy a more personal experience in a space that was even more welcoming. At least I hoped so.

I sent out what would now be my *eighth* announcement of a location change and hoped for the best.

***

The first client to walk through my door was Michael Banks, a prominent attorney and a partner at Morgan Lewis, one of Philadelphia's most prestigious law firms. I greeted him at the back entrance, and after a warm hello, I said "Since our last visit was at my 17th and Walnut Street store, I'm almost embarrassed to have you now be walking through my kitchen." And I still remember his response, "Hey Nance, It's 2008. Frugal is in. I'm happy to be here."

This theme also began to resonate with others. As I continued to actively connect with the clients I'd served in the past, they too returned, and in fact loved the warmth and ambience of the artistic studio that housed a service they had grown to appreciate.

A sales career can be an intense human experience because it allows you to share the lives of your clients in a personal way. **A good sales person will use this opportunity to engage in a way that makes a sale seem like more of a visit** than an exchange of goods and services.

I've been blessed to share professional relationships with many clients who have stayed with me from location to location over the past (to date) thirty-eight years. One such client is Bill Curtis, partner at Porter & Curtis, LLC Commercial Property & Casualty Brokers, who has been a constant source of support and now ranks as my longest standing client relationship. Bill's first custom shirt experience happened when he was just eighteen years old—thirty-six years later, he remains a loyal client and someone I value as a friend.

Dr. Peter Whybrow, who now lives in Los Angeles, is my longest standing *bespoke* client and is indeed one of just two remaining clients who prefer this service. He has his own hand drawn pattern and I personally cut each of his shirts, one at a time, as needed. I met him in 1982 at the tiny Locust Street studio I shared within the hair salon. His continued loyalty has graced our years together. (And he's amazing, as he's retained his same size over all these years. Who does that?)

Isaac (Ike) Barnes is also a client who has followed me from location to location, starting from my days at The John Shaw Company. He was in his twenties when we first started working together, and over the years we've developed a bond that continues to this day. When I told him I was writing this book, he coached me to continue and I mention him specifically because his friendship and support have been unwavering for over thirty years.

It is indeed the support of my clients that makes me look forward to each day, and now that I call myself "semi-retired," **I work at my own pace and I work only by appointment.**

Some years before, my daughter-in-law Merril urged me to turn my business into an appointment-only working model, and I railed against it. I was a retail business; this notion of hers seemed to contradict all the working principles I had followed for my entire working life. As a business owner, I felt I needed to be available in case I got a call. Some days were completely filled, yet on other days, the boredom of waiting for a client to drop by would only remind me that I was in scarcity mode.

**Every business should have an "open for business" schedule that best supports the product or service they sell.** My sons Bob and Ira are both PGA Golf Pros and it's a dawn to dusk commitment. My son Steve is a consultant and has weekends filled with conference calls and has more miles up in the air then most of his peers. My son Mitchell is an Executive Chef and starts his days earlier than most and ends when the job is done, and my daughter Lisa is Director of Sales for a design company and works where the job takes her. No two jobs are created equally **and when you're setting up your own business, you may want to create it in a way that supports your personal needs and wants.** Choosing a work model that includes time to *have a life* is way more fun than simply needing a money path to get your bills paid.

**I often wonder if this is the underlying principle of those who prefer to work for themselves, rather than be on-call to work the days and regular hours—and so often the extra hours—that a salaried position requires.**

My daughter-in-law Merril is a Food and Beverage Consultant who has a good sense of how service businesses operate. Her coaching from so many years ago has proven invaluable now.

**Perhaps there's a distinction for you to explore—are you intending to be a retail business or a service business?** When Merril originally made this suggestion, it was many years ago and had I followed it then, I think my days would have been filled with the feel-good experiences that now enhance my life, rather than the wasted hours that often brought fear and scarcity into my work day.

***

Chapter Recap: If the only reason you're in business is to make money, then the path will not be as joyful as the one that allows you to love what you do, helps you create the working relationships that enrich your life, and honors the lifestyle environment that provides the time to enjoy your successes.

CHAPTER

# Pay Yourself First

As of 2016, I've just celebrated my seventy-fifth birthday—and I'm still working.

I love what I do and my days are happily filled with purpose, but I work because I *must*. To date, my social security check is just six hundred and four dollars a month, and the only reason I even generate that amount is because it was calculated from my strongest working years at The Custom Shop, more than fifty years ago. I've worked hard all my life, yet now when income is so critical, I am still compelled to drive a salary to cover my most basic needs. Because I always paid myself *last*.

Don't ever do that.

**Always take a check, and always pay yourself *first*—**no matter what. I promise that once you've done that, you'll be more motivated to drive the income needed to pay the rest of your staff. More importantly, you'll be assured that you'll have a retirement income to fall back on when you need it most.

**It's important to get your personal operating behaviors in place as part of your early start- up thinking.** I never gave any thought to financial boundaries when I first opened the shop because I just wanted to get it *open,* and that set up a way of thinking that continues to this day.

\*\*\*

When I started the company, the kids and I were living off the balance of my house sale proceeds; the money from my ex-husband's financial agreement paid the salaries, but none for my own. As the company grew, my staff increased and the weekly salaries were often a struggle to pay. It was indeed a good week when I covered all the salary checks and got their taxes paid, yet there were some staff members whom I kept on payroll long after I should have, because I knew they needed the income.

Before I realized it, the years were passing and I was barely taking a weekly paycheck.

A by-product of this behavior is that I never included the costs of my time and talent when pricing my merchandise. I drove the company, but I was invisible. As I look back, **I note that the cost of our product never included the work I did in selling, marketing, bookkeeping, designing, pattern making, cutting, and the myriad of other daily tasks that kept the company viable.**

There never seemed a way for me to afford *me.*

**Always value yourself by putting a *value* on *yourself.*** No one should work for free, and *time is money.* As an entrepreneur, you may easily get sucked into doing everything possible to run your company by not taking a paycheck, or taking a limited amount. **Be conscious that if you start with this thinking, it could follow you for the balance of your working life.**

I now reflect that most of my peers have already retired, and many of my clients have aged out or passed away. The good news is that my health is strong, my genes belie my years, and my male clients have kids, so I'm now into a second generation of young men who want to wear custom shirts because their fathers did.

This story became real for me some years ago, when two young men came for shirts at my Ardmore studio.

I've always taken great pride in being able to make shirts that reflect a happy occasion, and while wedding shirts have always been a joy to make, the Bar Mitzvah shirt was always my favorite. Raising four sons, I was acutely aware that at thirteen years old, boys have a hard time being fitted. Their parents always planned ahead for their own outfits, but the clothing for their sons was expensive and difficult to size. At the time, I offered a Bar Mitzvah special for *Father and Son*, as I held it as a bonding experience, much the same way as the *Mother of the Bride* shares the excitement of choosing the wedding dress.

I advertised in *The Jewish Exponent*, a widely read Philadelphia newspaper. One of my Father/Son fittings had been for the Zinman family, well-known furriers in South Jersey. In that moment, I was wondering if the custom experience he was sharing with his dad seemed as "neat" to him at age thirteen as my seeing my Father's custom shirts with his cuff monogram was to me, when I was ten.

Twenty-something years later, two young men came in for fittings at my small Ardmore studio. As I was measuring one of them, he turned to his friend and said, "Have you ever been measured for custom shirts before?" "Not recently," he replied, "but I remember my dad took me with him to buy my Bar Mitzvah shirt. I was measured by a woman in New Jersey, and it really made me feel important." And all I remember saying was, "You're Zinman!!" These are the moments that brighten a day—these are the moments that matter.

Although this young man did order custom shirts, today's millennials aren't dressing the way their fathers did. The culture has changed and the market with it. This is an observation, not a complaint. I've adjusted my financial life to include this culture change because **change is the only thing you can depend on, and it's wise to include that in your thinking.**

Years ago, wearing custom shirts was a sign of affluence, of having made it. Today, it's a way to express individuality and to value craft. Meanwhile, on the "making a difference" side of things, my business has always provided shirts for people who can't get fit in standard sizes. I'm always gratified to be able to do this. I've measured skinny men with very long arms; men from three feet tall to seven feet three inches, athletes with overdeveloped muscles of the neck and shoulders; the hunchbacked, burn victims, amputees. In every economy, there will be people who value a custom fit, and I'm happy to provide this service. Yes, with a six hundred and four-dollar monthly social security payment, I still have to generate my own salary, but the truth is, I'd probably be doing it anyway.

Perhaps it's this small monthly check that keeps me in the game and gives me purpose, but I still insist: **"pay yourself *first*."** We're all wired differently, and what works for me by "living small" may be something that's not for you. Even if you're just making a limited income, keep a portion for yourself and start that 401K as soon as possible, because before you know it—you will need it.

*** 

---

> **Chapter Recap:** I'm thinking there are two main themes here: *Love* what you do, and pay yourself *first*.

---

# Afterword

―――――――――・・ﾟﾟﾟﾟﾟﾟﾟﾟﾟﾟﾟﾟﾟﾟ・―――――――――

## The Path Takes a Turn

### Health Crisis

What follows has been placed here as *Afterword*, although I wrote it in *real time* as I was already composing *Shirt Tales* in chronological order. I had started the *Tales* in late 2014 as a spare time project, writing when my schedule cleared. But on May 14th 2015 I hit a roadblock that rocked my world.

As part of my business behavior, I do everything I can to be pro-active about my health, and the last piece of my annual health check-up always includes the mammogram I get each year. Until May 14th, it was just an automatic test producing an automatic good reading.

But not this time.

I remember saying to the Assistant that the machine didn't *squish* me the way it usually does, and I was told it's a new 3D machine that takes a deeper photo cut than the machines used previously. It was far less uncomfortable, and I was told I'd get the results after the weekend.

No problem.

The test was on Thursday, and after enjoying a weekend time-off, I got a call from the hospital on Monday May 18th telling me that they wanted to do a re-test on May 20th, as there was something questionable in the results. I stared at the phone that had just delivered this crazy news and remember silently saying—"What?"—but all I could utter was, "I'll call for an appointment as soon as I return to my studio." I then zoned out, hung up, and sat in a stupor as I tried to assimilate this news that came at me so unexpectedly.

I have always enjoyed robust health, and "sick days" have only been reserved for those who work for me. **As the driver of my company, no business shows up unless I chase it down and being sick is not an option.**

Since 1978, I've been on the sales roller coaster that includes huge business volume on some days, and no business on others and while the ride is often exhilarating, it also includes days that are filled with palpitating stress. What would I do if I were really in the middle of a health crisis? I was now fast-tracking to do everything I could, as quickly as I could, to get to the other side of this crazy and unexpected news.

**I recognized that Pro-Active behavior has always been a life choice for me,** and now more than ever, I was committed to achieving a positive result.

**On Wednesday May 20th** I received a second mammogram and a follow-up ultra-sound.

**On Thursday May 21st** I met my surgeon who advised me there was a calcification that signaled the presence of cancer, and it should be removed by a lumpectomy.

**On Wednesday May 27th** I was asked to return to the office for surgery prep and pre-testing.

**On Friday May 29th** I was at the hospital for the planting of a radio-active seed that would identify the surgery site.

**On Tuesday June 2rd** I had my pre-operation interview, requested my anesthesia choice and was given instructions about the sterile wash that needed to be done that night, and again the following morning.

**Wednesday June 3rd**—surgery day.

My oldest son, Steve, took me to the surgery center and stayed with me until the procedure started. My surgeon was wonderful, my recovery was easy and the operation went successfully. As someone with very low blood pressure, I always opt out of general anesthesia when possible and my instructions were carefully followed.

My Doctor, W. Bradford Carter, said he had removed everything at the site that was questionable and the margins were clear. He was confident that the surgery produced the result for which we had all been hoping, and I was discharged to continue my healing until we met again to discuss next steps.

My cousin Rae Roeder drove me home and brought the traditional chicken soup that is a *Jewish staple* in getting someone back to good health, and she stayed with me until I was comfortable being on my own. When she left, the house was quiet and I found myself meditating as I often do when life comes at me so fast. In the stillness of my home, I noted that family is everything. It's not possible to go through a health issue without their support, and I was now reminded of it in a way I had never before experienced. My family is large, I was exhausted, and I felt the best way to let everyone know my progress was to write a combined email to all, as I was too tired for one-on-one phone support.

**Blessings in one's life are often taken for granted**—but not this time.

As I started writing the contact line, I noted how many names I had listed as family and close friends. I don't think I ever recognized or even acknowledged this network of support until I saw the contact line fill up with the people with whom I share my life. With five children and five grandchildren, friends who are *family* to me, and friends who have been longstanding, the list was mind-blowing. **Yes—I am blessed. And it took a health crisis to really "get" that at a level I had never experienced before.**

**On Friday June 5th**, I felt strong enough to drive to our family's weekend retreat and planned to stay there and recuperate. I hung out with some of

123

my kids and by Sunday night the place was again quiet as everyone left to start their work week. Whatever discomfort I felt was being handled by pain meds and I was sure I'd be ok until I returned the following afternoon. As I prepared for bed, I took another pain pill and spent what soon became a sleep experience that culminated in excruciating pain at the surgery site. When I awoke the next morning, my wound was seeping through my sleeping bra, night shirt and sheet, and my breast was bright red.

I was an hour away from the hospital, so I quickly closed the house down and went directly to my Doctor's office, located on the hospital grounds. My surgeon was unable to see me as he had been called to complete his Reserve Duty as part of his Armed Forces commitment, but I was seen by his partner, Dr. Thomas Frazier who was handling his patients as well as his own. I was ushered into the exam room and found myself in the presence of this warm and wonderful man who explained I had a staph infection that was causing my pain. He assured me that antibiotics would soon alleviate the symptoms and he would be the one to monitor my healing until the infection cleared.

In harsh situations one can sometimes find a moment of mirth, and as I was sitting on the table with an open gown and a seeping breast, I noticed a small monogram on the top of his pocket and I remember saying," Ahh— that looks like a custom shirt to me. I'm a custom shirtmaker, perhaps we can do some business together?" I then reached over and took a business card from my wallet and left it on the exam table. Yes. I really did that, and yes—he is now my client.

As I recall this memory, I'm aware that in business, **"one should never lose an opportunity to do a commercial."** (This was a favorite phrase often used by my friend and colleague Alphonse Pignataro, and I have successfully lived into that since I first heard it in 1985.) **Every day, in every way, when you are your business, there are always ways you can share who you are and what you do.** This may have been an odd place and time, but the behavior was simply automatic and the doctor was happily open to the suggestion.

What follows is a recap that was presented as a July 8th, 2015 publishing post on *LinkedIn*. What transpired after I left the Surgeon's office changed my life, and I took the opportunity to share the insight that made such a difference. Although it was a more personal story than usually presented on a business networking site, I hoped that the breakthrough I had experienced might have some value for the other entrepreneurs who spend their days (and some nights) grinding out an income as they chase after their future in the pursuit of a more meaningful life.

\*\*\*

# A CEO's Unexpected Wake-up Call (Enough is Enough)

## By Nancy Gold, Business Owner, Media Consultant, and Entrepreneurial Coach

*Whether you're a man or a woman, at some point you may experience the phone call that changes your business thinking. The call I received was my life-changer, and what follows brought clarity to my life and a renewed sense of purpose.*

*The shift happened on May 14th, when my annual mammogram produced the call-back I had never anticipated, and I was terrified by the news. The re-test happened a few days later; and by June 3rd, I was at the hospital for a lumpectomy. The surgery was completely successful, but I experienced a staph infection at the surgery site, and due to an allergic reaction to three of the antibiotics, it took almost three weeks to clear. While most of the time is still a blur, this four-week assault on my life left me free to explore my innermost thoughts and feelings, and the end game has been surprising.*

*While I could offer this was one of the worst months of my life, it also rolled out as a breakthrough month that altered my thinking and changed my life.*

*In business, we speak about creating that important Network that helps you get noticed for either your product, or the kudos you wish to share. When your health is on the line, that network can also serve to remind you of the friendships you've created, and the clients who hold you as more than a resource… at least, that's how it occurred for me.*

*These connections buoyed my spirits and reminded me of what's truly important: Good Health trumps EVERYTHING.*

*When you see who you are, reflected back to you through the comments and connections in your life, you can cut through the minutia that you hold as important, even as you slog through your business day.*

*For me, part of that load has always been the stress attached to driving that next project or creating the money flow needed to protect my company. As an entrepreneur, many are dependent upon the product I deliver or the service I render. I'm a Master Shirtmaker who has been on this treadmill of choice since 1978 as CEO of The King's Collar Shirtmakers, and since 2000, as the driver of my business support company, The King's Writer.*

*When projects go smoothly and sales are booming, I am always gratified by the results; but when I hit a wall and everything stops, I feel like I'm losing my business and I will never recover. My work life has always been a series of incredible highs and gut-wrenching lows, and the ride has been exhausting.*

*As I look back, I am still astonished that I survived September 11, 2001, or the market meltdown and our national crisis in 2008-2009, but my companies remain intact. In order for this to happen, I took the necessary steps that would permit me to live and work more simply. I bought a commercial building that allowed me to give up a rental lease, stopped carrying inventory, moved into an "appointment only" business concept, and focused on providing the best service I could offer.*

*It was a good plan, but it was still a plan that came from scarcity, and stress is almost always scarcity's partner.*

*On June 6th, just days after my surgery, I experienced a massive staph infection that brought me to the Surgeon's office for treatment, and created a window of time when working was not an option. When this unexpected "sabbatical" occurred, I was not prepared for it, and that's when the fear surfaced.*

*I found myself sliding into pessimism and questioning my ability to keep my business going. I felt that if I could no longer drive my income, I would never have enough to cover my personal needs and my financial responsibilities. Every possible negative thought took me to the place in my head that said, "It's OVER".*

*And then two days later, I opened up my business email site and there were two clients I had not heard from for almost ten years. They wanted an appointment the following week for a shirt fitting, and that's when the breakthrough happened.*

*I am my company, and with a 38-year history, <u>I noted that my company</u> <u>would only cease to exist when I said so;</u> it would have nothing to do with market forces. I was the indeed the driver of my business future, only now I could do it on my terms. I recognized that my fear of loss was always tied to outside forces and since I'd already created a safety net that contained my costs, I could easily kick back and enjoy the life I had worked so hard to create. I could take a day off. I could take a long weekend. I could hang with my grandkids. I could put stress away, replace it with living full-out, knowing that I had already planted the seeds that would bring the fruit to harvest.*

*My new bottom line? I am an appointment-only business, and I can shape my life around the company and not have the company shape my life.*

*Wow.*

*Perhaps this post is more personal than most, but I've written it in real time, and if I've given just one person a small insight into how a breakdown can create a breakthrough, then the story was worth sharing. For me, it was certainly worth writing just to reinforce the insight, and notice that it has actually taken hold.*

*I have a long time client, Dr. Marshall Pressman, who closes his phone message with the words "Carpe Diem." This directive now has new meaning for me.*

*end of post*

\*\*\*

- - - - - - - - - - - - - - - - - - - - - - - - - - - - - - - - - - - - - - - - -

<u>Chapter Recap</u>: A life-altering insight can often occur in the midst of a breakdown. When you live in the moment and trust a higher power, there's always an answer.

- - - - - - - - - - - - - - - - - - - - - - - - - - - - - - - - - - - - - - - - -

If you've reached this last page, then you're already on the "ledge" and getting started will simply take a leap of faith. *Trust yourself*—**"Go for it!"**

As the author of this book, I now find *myself* traveling down a new path I had not envisioned when I started writing the original *Business Manual*. Yes, I am a Master Shirtmaker, yet I'm also a writer. **Some people box themselves into a career path that gives them no space to explore their other skills.**

I'm suggesting that this path is generally driven by the education one receives and the expertise one develops as the information is integrated. It occurs to me that a *gift* comes more naturally and is usually powered by something you love to do.

Very few of us are one dimensional, and many excel in different areas of our lives. Perhaps it's time to value and appreciate your skills, while also finding the time to include the *gifts* you possess that add flavor and substance to the lives of those with whom you interact. You can be an actor *and* a painter, a ballplayer *and* a brilliant businessman, an Executive Director of a Foundation *and* a gifted photographer—and you can derive an income from both.

My best wishes for your success and happiness, and may you make a difference in the lives of others—because as an entrepreneur—YOU WILL.

Big hug,

Nancy

# Appendix

**This is how it gets done:**
# The Business Manual: The *Road Map* for a Start-up

I trust you have gleaned some useful insights from the tales I have shared, and possibly a catalyst that allows you to follow your *own* dream.

This book actually evolved after creating the document below that was meant to assist my entrepreneurial business clients. I was going to post it on *LinkedIn* when my sister Joan said, "Why? Why post it for one day when what you really have are the stories behind all of the coaching steps presented in your manual. You need to write a book and include it at the back."

—And that's exactly what I did.

*The Business Manual* follows and I hope the content will ease your way as you consider the possibility of driving your own future. In today's changing economy, I'm now thinking that the best business opportunity is the one that you alone control.

**"You are the captain of your own ship; don't let anyone else take the wheel."**

**- Michael Josephson**

\*\*\*

# THE BUSINESS MANUAL

I am about to provide you with an enormous amount of information. Prior to reading through this Business Manual, I caution you to remember just one word before starting down any start-up path: —*Prioritize.*

As a new business, each day will hold an issue or a task that can seem overwhelming. When you find you've reached your saturation point, consider *stopping.* Mistakes can happen when your mind is on overload and your body is tired, and an error in judgment can be costly—a clear head allows for a smarter decision and a new day will give you better perspective.

***

**The most important advice is to LOVE what you do**. If it's just a "job," and not your life purpose, you may easily resent the long hours, financial pressure and emotional connections that are part of growing *any* business.

## GETTING STARTED

(and *yes,* you'll need a business plan.)

- **Build a spread-sheet that includes your estimated start-up costs.** How much do you expect to generate for the first year? How much for subsequent years? Do you have the staying power to grow your business, regardless of outside influences?

- **Most businesses require at least three years to get their direction solid.** The first year is your *work-in-progress* where you iron out the unexpected. If the first year ends in a comfort zone, your second year can provide some exciting results.

- **Be very careful about making costly purchases in the third year,** as this is often the time when inappropriate financial choices are made. Always spend smartly, and never let your ego rule you, even when it looks like you're in positive financial territory.

- **Does the idea have "legs?"** Is there additional income that can be generated by internet sales, is there a franchising possibility, and will you be building something that has a business re-sale value?

- **Explore Loan Programs.** There is often funding available for minority-owned businesses, as well as loans to veterans and woman-owned businesses.

**Get your business name and your logo solid.** Your business name should easily identify your service or product. It is the critical first step of *branding* your business identity. **Don't be afraid of hiring professionals to assist you with this, as this expense could be your most important purchase.**


# FINANCIAL SUPPORT

- *Before* you apply for a line of credit, check your personal credit report for any errors that may hurt your financing efforts.

- **Make sure you bring your own start-up capital to the table, and most importantly, always ask your bank or backers for more than you need**; this added safety net is often the critical piece that can protect your *original* investment, and can be an insurance policy that helps you survive your first year.

- **Be very careful about taking on partners.** If all you need is the use of their money, it's often a better idea to pay the interest on a loan and own 100 percent of the company. Giving away a percentage of your business is often too high a price to pay for access to capital, and **resentment can easily surface if you're doing all the work and having all the responsibility.**

- **In a privately held business, always ask for overdraft protection for at least one thousand dollars.** This is over and above your line of credit, and most banks will have no problem with an amount this small. With bank fees so costly and business credit so valuable, protecting your checkbook balance protects your bank account *and* your good name. As there's sometimes the possibility of accepting an NSF check, and there's often a delay in posting credit card charges, you may not have the balance necessary to cover your business checks on the date they appear.

**From this point on, I've included check boxes to help you hold your vision and consider the action steps presented:**

## Legal Costs:

- ☐ **It is critical to work with an attorney when you begin exploring how best to set up your legal and financial obligations.** Your attorney and your accountant can both explain the differences between Partnerships, LLC's, Professional Corporations, and Sole Proprietor designations, and can point you in the right direction. Every business is different, so make sure you have the correct legal fit.

- ☐ Do not enter into a lease agreement unless it is carefully reviewed by your attorney, and if you're not comfortable with negotiations, have your lawyer hammer out an agreement that offers your best opportunity for success. **The best leases are top heavy and bottom light.**

- ☐ **Ask for a lower yearly rent that rises as your profits increase.** (If the rent is set, try to start paying the bigger percentage in year three.)

☐ Always consider starting with at least a five-year lease, with a five-year option. There's no reason to put your time, effort, creativity, and funding into anything shorter.

☐ If possible, be wary about triple net leases; try to keep your rent as easy as possible without needing to share your gross income or cover additional building costs.

**Get an Accountant:** (Keep your business liabilities and financial responsibilities separate from your personal debt; *never* **sign personally for a business debt**.)

☐ Work with your accountant to explore organizational costs that include the best tax shelter possible.

☐ An LLC might seem like an easy way to start a business, but the tax liability can *crush* you, if you start making a lot of money. The more money you make, the more you're taxed, and a Professional Corporation may allow you to hold on to more income. There is also a distinction between an S Corp and a C Corp, and you and your advisor(s) should discuss your best option.

**Operating Costs**

☐ **Check out your business liability insurance options.** Always make sure you protect your life's assets by having appropriate coverage.

☐ Pay *yourself* FIRST! **Get into the habit of it.** As a proprietor-owned business, you'll need that financial history for when you retire and collect benefits.

☐ **Any dated bills that may cause you a late fee if delayed, should be handled as an "automatic" payment that hits your bank statement on its due date.** It's the best way to keep your credit clean.

## Don't be afraid to hire a Consultant

Any new business should consider using a consultant to help them walk through the mine fields. **Paying for a good consultant, just like paying a good sales person, is not an expense—it's an insurance policy.**

When you hire someone who's good at what they do, the money you pay is more than compensated by the money they save you, or in the case of a salesperson, the added income they generate. **When staff is talented, they basically drive their own income by the added dollars they generate that helps to build your business.**

☐ If marketing is not your strong suit, make sure you hire someone who has the credentials to do it for you. **There is a difference between PR and Marketing:** Marketing establishes your company once it's operating by continually creating its brand, and PR is the ongoing attention needed to put (and keep) that brand out to the public.)

☐ Start thinking about a web site: Check URL access for future web business and business identity, and consider a consultant to help you with the design. There are inexpensive web site programs available, but *do not* skimp on the narrative that tells your story. **Hire a professional web site writer** if this is not your strong suit.

☐ If media is needed, find a media buyer who can guide you on the best path to get your message heard. Radio ads, TV spots, or Print ads all work, and some better than others, depending on the service or product you provide.

## Business Location

Explore the demographics that will support your product or service. Think about your product and its target audience. Will its location drive new customers to its establishment? Does it match your product offering? Is the address easily recognizable?

☐ If you're a "destination-driven business," you can often save rental dollars by finding a location with which people are familiar. A second floor, or rear location in a well-known area, can keep your rental costs more manageable, yet be just as effective.

☐ If you're a "high-profile business," a higher rent district might actually serve you better, as marketing and advertising might be more cost effective for a better location than the money you save by paying less rent in a less attractive location.

☐ Consider an address that's near your competition (if your product or service warrants this.) There's always a shared audience when you're near someone with a similar product, and it's your chance to *piggyback* on the advertising they pay for their own location.

☐ See if accessible parking is close by, check township rules for tow-away zones if near your location, and make sure you share parking issues with your clients/customers. **Nothing loses a client faster than having their car towed.**

**Sharing space:** You may also want to consider "sharing" a space with a business that can offer support for your product. Often this shared location gives *both* retailers added coverage, lower expenses for each, cross marketing options, and a captive audience that allows clients and customers from each entity to have other convenient options from which to choose.

**Kiosk Possibilities:** A mall location may work well, but weekly hours can be hard to manage.

**Storefront vs. office location**: depending on your product and/or service, **an office location, or upper floor can work for an *appointment only* business,** and the operating costs are usually much less.

**Web-based Businesses:** Sometimes your business can be done from your home. Check into the possibilities that *Etsy* and *Pinterest* offer.

\*\*\*

# Start-up Costs

## Costs to Consider:

- ☐ Rent (plus deposit)

- ☐ Utilities (plus deposit)

- ☐ Payroll

- ☐ Support Services: legal/ accounting/web design

- ☐ Inventory: (terms are usually net 30)

- ☐ Product samples, display material and store "furniture"

- ☐ Security System/Cameras/Alarms

- ☐ Business License

- ☐ Internet/ Phone/Fax/ (with answering machine

- ☐ Insurance

- ☐ Gift Certificates/Sales slips/Tags/Bags/Tissue/Boxes/Business Cards

- ☐ Computer/Printer/Fax

- ☐ Bookkeeping

- ☐ Legal

- ☐ Advertising, (Local Newspaper/Postcards/Radio/Mailer/Email like *Constant Contact*)

- ☐ Merchant Services/Banking

- ☐ Benefit Packages

# Getting the Business Up and Running

**Always check with your local government about their zoning regulations before you commit to a lease,** and also be clear about the outside signage regulations in your town before you think about your window treatments.

- [ ] **Make sure your partnership agreement is fair and balanced.**

- [ ] **Be wary about "handshake" agreements**—a "change of mind" can put your business at risk, as well as the possibility of a legal challenge and its costs to defend. Trust between parties/partners may be obvious during early stages, but remember to put your agreements in writing and make sure you get legal oversight for all signed documents.

- [ ] What are you selling? What kind of inventory do you need to carry?

- [ ] Know **everything** about the product you sell.

- [ ] Think about *inside* store signage.

- [ ] Order your Labels, Tags, Signs, Gift Certificates and Register Forms.

- [ ] Get Business Cards and Stationary. (What would we ever do without *Vistaprint?*)

- [ ] Establish the "theme" of your store; how will you be presenting your product?

- [ ] Line up vendors.

- [ ] Get your merchant services account activated. (As rates are always variable, you'll want to "shop" for your best service provider.)

- [ ] Check out trade show dates, if applicable.

- ☐ Think about opening PR—(Possibly tying into a Charity Event.)

- ☐ Think about store hours, and extra staffing if needed. (Part-time saves additional costs for benefits.)

- ☐ Spec out your retail neighbors and do comparison shopping for price points.

- ☐ Establish a method for reflecting daily sales for year to year comparisons.

- ☐ Establish and use an operating document to keep your business running smoothly. **Write up your Employee Manual.** Company rules should include dress codes, vacation and personal days and a non-compete clause, if the company so warrants.

- ☐ Think about expensing your own auto and health benefits as a company perk.

- ☐ **Establish a method for capturing client names for follow-up contact** and sale announcements. In my company, I use *Constant Contact*, and I make sure I reach out to my base monthly.

- ☐ **Start to collect a list of every resource you use** to make or sell your product, and the names and companies of those who handle any repairs that could slow down your business, if faced with an emergency. (This is your *Go-To* list.)

- ☐ Your mailing list is your company's Bible. *Never* **share this list for any purpose**—(Customers need to trust that their information is safely held.)

- ☐ Speak to the "listening" of your audience—don't be an intrusion in their day.

- ☐ Make sure you only contact your clients when you have something of value to share.

- ☐ Say "Thank you" to those who support you by buying your goods and/or services.

- ☐ **Always be your word.** When you say you're going to do something—Do it. If you've promised a deadline—Keep it. If delayed, be courteous and let your client/or purveyor know that.

**In advertising, always remember "The rule of three."** No one sees just one ad, or hears just one radio spot. Repetition is the key to success, and **you need to start with at least *three* buys, in order for anyone to remember they heard you the *first* time.**

- ☐ Think about where you'll be advertising (and the best media opportunity to consider.)

- ☐ **Always use your consultants to help you negotiate the best deal**, as well as helping you with your copy material. (**Find a good business writer** to help you with copy if this is not a strong suit for you.)

## Fit Out:

(You sometimes get lucky by finding a storefront with some amenities, which will help to minimize these expenses.)

- ☐ Walls/Carpet/Décor

- ☐ Store furniture and Mirrors

- ☐ Counters

- ☐ Dressing room (if retail fashion)

- ☐ Displays/Hangers (Various sizes)/Mannequins/Shelving (if retail fashion)

- [ ] Signage/Window & Indoor/Window Trim/POP Signs

- [ ] Cash Register

- [ ] Computer Support/POS

- [ ] Sound System/Flat Screens (A possible future expense)

- [ ] Lighting/Electrical/Telephone Wiring

- [ ] Bathroom Décor/Signage (Bathrooms may have to be ADA accessible)

- [ ] Iron and clothes steamer on premises (any clothing store)

- [ ] Providing a space for employees to eat-in is a welcome and cost-saving amenity. The Hospitality Area should include table, chairs, refrigerator and coffee station.

- [ ] If food service is offered by your business, check zoning to see if outside tables are allowed.

**Check for fire safety regulations:**

- [ ] Have back-up extinguishers and first aid supplies accessible.

**Make sure Rest rooms are *clean*.**

- [ ] If someone needs to use your facilities, **be gracious and let them.**

## Store Operation Practices:

- [ ] Have your store display windows done professionally if you can't do them yourself and change at least every three weeks. (Every two weeks is ideal.)

☐ Answer your phones by time of day greeting and store name, and **smile when speaking, as it reflects well to the listener.**

☐ When you leave a phone or cell message, **repeat your number twice** so people can avoid hearing your announcement again—they'll appreciate this time saving courtesy.

☐ **Use music as background, and choose your format wisely.** What you play should support the product you sell. (Soft jazz and classical always works for upscale clientele, while rap or rock music appeals to a younger audience.)

☐ Greet a customer *as soon* as they enter your shop or facility: "Hello, may I help you?" Don't hover—give them space, (but don't neglect them.)

☐ Offer packaging that makes your product stand out from your competitors, and if the product warrants, offer a *Free* gift wrapping service.

☐ First Aid and CPR support: Make sure you or your staff members have the ability to address a medical emergency should one arise.

☐ Know about your parking regulations and suggest the closest place they can use.

☐ Make sure you have a handy list of any emergency phone numbers you may need.

☐ Become a resource for any question a customer may have, **and if they want something you don't carry, tell them who does.** (*Keeping it on the block* is a great community builder.)

☐ The most important product you can offer is *Great Service.* **Never make a customer wrong**—(even if they are.) They'll appreciate the "pass" and it prompts them to speak well of you to others.

☐ Have your merchandise clearly marked for price. Someone may *actually* be able to afford it, but may be too embarrassed to ask.

☐ Change displays often. They won't get stale for customers, but they'll get stale for you and that affects your selling personality.

☐ Keep your merchandise neat, and re-fold or re-stock as soon as possible. Small and repetitive inventories make a poor presentation.

☐ Keep your store spotless and dust free.

**If you're a storefront business, be sure your windows are *fabulous*.** A great window creates a new or returning customer.

☐ Do not place any posters on your windows.

☐ Get your storefront windows washed and cleaned on a regular basis.

☐ **Leave some store lights on at night** as this offers a welcoming view of your inventory and surroundings during off hours. "Window Shopping" adds interest for your goods and services when you are *not* open for business.

**Do your "homework" and know everything about the products you sell.**

☐ Nothing instills more confidence than sales associates who know what they're talking about and can answer any questions that may come up.

☐ **Strive to make multiple sales from the same customer.** Don't be an order taker. Sometimes, all you need to say is **"how many would you like?"**

☐ Establish a formula for paying your sales associates that encourages them to perform at their highest level—*and be generous.* **Good**

**sales people, just as good consultants, are *never* an expense—** they are the assets that drive *your* income.

☐ Never allow your NEED to keep a sales associate outweigh your ability to pay them—I offer this statement with all due respect, but **sometimes the market rate of a job is what sets its salary.**

***

---

> <u>**Chapter Recap:**</u> **Create a business that has value and can be sold if circumstances warrant this decision.** At the very least, create an asset that can be continued by a partner or a family member should this concept be needed or desired.

---

**In Closing:** I trust I have offered information that will allow you to start well and continue with confidence. You are about to embark on a life journey that will have its ups and downs, and the most important advice I can give is to just ride through them and stay pro-active. The worst thing that ever happened to me *always* preceded the magical experience that followed, and I've learned to just wait for the gift—and then get back into action.

*"Faith is believing in something that doesn't exist for us yet."*

—Mark Waldman

# More Information

If you would like additional copies of this book for gifts, school, or organization, please contact Orders@TheKingsWriter.com and we will arrange for billing and shipping. Credit Card services are available for Visa, Mastercard, American Express, and Discover. You may also order from the Lulu.com Bookstore under Business & Economics category. For more information about the writing services we offer, please contact Nancy@ TheKingsWriter.com, and if you would like a book reading or a private presentation to your group, please contact us through our web site below:

www.TheKingsWriter.com

Thank you for considering the information I have presented, and for taking the time to reflect upon its possibilities. To have a strong economy, courageous entrepreneurs are needed to lead the way, and the concept or service you offer can make a local difference.

I urge you to support the small businesses who provide a product or service that is MADE IN AMERICA. While this may be "the road less traveled", as more folks take this path and also try to SHOP LOCAL, the more our National economy will grow.

*** 

*In most books, the I, or first person, is omitted. We commonly do not remember that it is, after all, always the first person that is speaking. I should not talk so much about myself if there were anybody else whom I knew as well. Unfortunately, I am confined to this theme by the narrowness of my experience. Moreover, I, on my side, require of every writer, first or last, a simple and sincere account of his own life, and not merely what he has heard of other men's lives; some such account as he would send to his kindred from a distant land; for if he had lived sincerely, it must have been in a distant land to me. Perhaps these pages are more particularly addressed to poor students. As for the rest of my readers, they will accept such portions as apply to them. I trust none will stretch the seams in putting on the coat, for it may do good service to him whom it fits.*

*___ Henry David Thoreau*